Herm

aux Rats
Oyster Point
Shell Beach
Le Plat Houmet
Herm Common
Shell Bay
Neolithic Graves
Bear's Beach
Herm
Hermetier
Belvoir Bay
Caquorobert
Herm Harbour
St Tugual
6 Le Manor
White House Hotel
Putraine
Rosaire Steps
Mouette
Selle Roque
Crevichon
Le Creux Pigeon
Jethou
Grande Fauconnière

0   500 m
0   500 yds

N

Pembroke Bay
L'Ancresse Bay
Fontenelle Bay
Beaucette Marina
L'Ancresse Common
La Fontenelle
Le Béhus Dolmen
Le Grand Havre
Vale
Clos du Valle
Hommet Paradis
Bordeaux
Pétils Bay
Guernsey Freesia Centre
Vale Castle
Bordeaux Bay
Oatlands Village
St Sampson
St Sampson Bay
Guernsey Candles
St Sampson
Château des Marais (Ivy Castle)
Spur Point
Belle Grève Bay

5
4
St Peter Port
1
3 **2**
Castle Cornet
Havelet Bay
lle au Roi
Aquarium
Les Terres Point
herine t Studio
tin's Church
Village de Putron
Fermain Point
Fermain Bay
Sausmarez Manor
Doyle Monument
Moulin Huet Bay
St Martin's Point Telegraph Bay
Jerbourg Point

Bec du Nez
Eperquerie Common
Les Fontaines
Noire Pierre
Petite Moie
Saignie Bay
Window in the Rock
La Tour
Port du Moulin
La Grève de la Ville
Point Robert
Grande Moie
La Seigneurie Gardens
German Occupation & Heritage Museum
Port à la Jument
Island Hall
M
Maseline Harbour
Brecqhou
Big Sark
St Peter's
7
Gouliot Passage
Jail
Creux Harbour
Les Lâche
Havre Gosselin
Pilcher Monument
Caves de Victor Hugo
Petit Derrible Bay
Porte és Saies
Derrible Bay
Dixcart Bay
Point Chateau
Derrible Point
La Pointe de la Joue
Grande Grève
La Coupée
Baleine
Adonis Headland
Roug Câne Bay

Sark

0   1000 m
0   1000 yds

N

INSIGHT GUIDES

Great Breaks

GUERNSEY

Contents

Walks and Tours

Travel Tips

Guernsey's Top 10

The Channel Islands of Guernsey, Herm, Sark and Alderney bask in a temperate climate off the French coast, combining British sensibility with continental sunshine in what is the last remnant of the Duchy of Normandy.

▲ **St Peter Port** *(p.14)*. Explore this ancient port with its cobbled streets, colourful harbour and fine seafood restaurants.

▲ **German Occupation Museum** *(p.45)*. See how the islanders lived during World War II, through recreated domestic scenes, documents, recipes and ration books.

▲ **Castle Cornet** *(p.18)*. Listen to the roar of the noon-day gun and explore the museums of this medieval castle.

▶ **Hauteville House** *(p.24)*. Take a tour of Victor Hugo's home in exile and discover that the French author was also an inspired interior decorator.

▼ **Herm** (p.72). Take a day or half-day trip to this tiny, car-free island and enjoy the walks, beaches and birdlife.

▲ **Sausmarez Manor** (p.41). Tour the historic family manor, explore informal gardens and discover more than 200 works of art in the sculpture park.

▼ **La Seigneurie, Sark** (p.88). Enjoy the formal walled garden and exotic shrubbery at La Seigneurie, home of the seigneur of Sark since 1730.

▲ **Fort Grey** (p.47). Gripping stories of shipwrecks around Guernsey's western shores are the theme of the museum within the fort.

▼ **St Anne, Alderney** (p.96). An engaging little town with cobbled streets, pastel-painted old houses and a fascinating small museum.

▲ **Folk and Costume Museum** (p.65). Intriguing displays from rural 18th century life, housed in farm buildings around a central courtyard.

Overview

Guernsey

Guernsey and its tiny sister islands lie in the Gulf of St Malo and have a distinct Gallic twist. Expect beautiful bays, superb seafood and the sunniest climate in the British Isles

When French novelist Victor Hugo was exiled in 1851, he thought long and hard about where to make his new home. Since he spoke only French, he wanted to live somewhere where French was understood.

He finally chose the Channel Islands because they were 'morsels of France fallen into the sea and gathered up by England'.

If Hugo felt perfectly at home in the Channel Islands, so did the numerous British and Irish army officers and colonial servants who chose to settle here in the 19th century. The addition of new Anglian and Celtic ingredients to the existing French culture resulted in a mix that makes the islands feel reassuringly familiar, yet still exotic.

'Similar but different' is a phrase that could also describe the way that Jersey and Guernsey seek to differentiate themselves from each other. They each issue their own currencies, phonecards and postage stamps, none of which are valid on the mainland.

Letter boxes are different colours (red on Jersey, blue on Guernsey) and each claims its version of the classic knitted fisherman's jumper. Guernsey people rarely refer to Jersey by name: to them, it is 'the other island'. They refer to its inhabitants, only half in jest, as *crapauds* (toads) – because the toad is found on Jersey but not on Guernsey. With their slower pace of life Guernsey people are dismissed as *ânes* (donkeys) by their bigger-island rivals.

LOCATION AND CLIMATE

As a group the islands sit just off the Cherbourg peninsula. With an area of 24 sq miles (62 sq km), and a population of around 63,000 Guernsey is the second biggest of the Channel Islands after Jersey, but the more densely populated. The Bailiwick of Guernsey consists of Guernsey, the islands of Herm, Jethou, Sark and Alderney, and a number of scattered lighthouse rocks and islets, such as Burhou, Ortac and the Casquets. The tiny islands of Herm (20 minutes by ferry) and Sark

Above: white sands of Mouisonniere Beach, Herm. **Below**: walking down Pier Steps in St Peter Port.

Above: Alderney's Mannez Lighthouse has great views from its lantern.

(45 minutes) are peaceful retreats, with sandy beaches and dramatic clifftop scenery. Sark's 450-year-old feudal system came to an end in 2008 when the Chief Pleas (legislative body) was reformed, the first general election was held and Sark became Europe's newest democracy. Alderney is the northernmost of the Channel Islands, just 8 miles (13km) from France. It was deliberately depopulated during the war, and used as a forced labour camp. Community life has been successfully rebuilt since the island's liberation in 1945; Alderney is now popular with ornithologists and beach lovers looking for privacy and a peaceful escape from the busy world.

The Channel Islands are mild in winter and sunny in summer, but strong winds can make temperatures feel cool. In the summer months the islands have a daily average of eight hours of sunshine and an average maximum temperature of 68°F (20°C). The Atlantic sea temperatures are cool for swimming, averaging 62.8°F (17.1°C) in summer.

BRITISH LINKS

Although they are not truly British, the Channel Islands have been linked with the British Crown for over 900 years. Self-government was granted to the islands by King John in 1204, as a reward for staying loyal to the English Crown after the rest of Normandy was conquered by King Philippe II of France. Ever since the islands have pledged allegiance to the English Crown, and as the last remaining territories of the dukes of Normandy, they toast the Queen of England as 'Our Duke of Normandy'. The islands delegate matters of foreign policy and defence to the UK parliament, but in all other affairs – especially in taxation and financial policy – they guard their independence zealously.

ECONOMY

Guernsey saw major changes during the late 20th century as the financial services industry took over from agriculture and tourism as the mainstay of the economy. The sector is now completely dominant, generating about 40 percent of the island's economic output and £105 million a year in tax. The almost complete absence of taxes on capital makes the islands very attractive to wealthy incomers, and to the banking community. Traditional activities such as dairy farming and fishing still continue and recent years have seen a surge in small-scale producers such as cheese-makers, organic farmers and specialist pig breeders.

Tourism saw its heyday in the 1950s and 1960s when railway workers flocked over with their free ferry tickets. Today the emphasis is on up-market short breaks, heritage,

F Tides

The islands have one of the largest tidal movements in the world; the change between high and low water almost doubles the size of the islands. Powerful tides expose huge areas of rock pools and clean, sandy and rarely crowded beaches. Fishermen forage along the foreshore for the lobsters, mussels, clams and oysters that end up being served as *plateaux de fruits de mer* in the island's many seafood restaurants.

Above: the seawall protects the shoreline and town.

gastronomy and traditional leisure activities. And Guernsey wants to keep it that way, with no theme parks and no Starbucks. Numbers of overnight visitors have dropped in the last year or so but day visitor numbers have been boosted by visiting cruiseships.

ENVIRONMENT

The coastal fringes have their own distinctive wildlife, from the puffins and gannets that nest on the offshore islets, to the sea kale, horned poppy and sea holly that grows on the dunes. On Guernsey the island of Lihou and nearby nature reserves have been designated as a Ramsar site (a wetland of international importance). This large intertidal zone has a rich biodiversity of flora and fauna.

Guide to Coloured Boxes

E Eating	This guide is dotted with coloured boxes providing additional practical and cultural information to make the most of your visit. Here is a guide to the coding system.
F Fact	
G Green	
K Kids	
S Shopping	
V View	

Green lanes on Guernsey, called Ruettes Tranquilles, have reduced the speed limit on country lanes to 15mph (24kph) and encourage cyclists and pedestrians. On the other hand, Guernsey has one of the highest car ownership rates in the world, and the amount of traffic and parking problems may deter you from driving.

Above: cycling is the main form of transport on Sark.

Food and Drink

Guernsey has a thriving gastronomic scene, particularly in St Peter Port. The clear, warm waters around the island produce an abundance of shellfish, including scallops, lobsters and crabs. Eating out is an essential part of life on the island, and with its many wealthy residents, Guernsey has more than its fair share of up-market restaurants. Even the discerning French come across the Channel to indulge their palates. But at the other end of the scale, there are plenty of humble establishments, from fish and chip cafés and ethnic restaurants to rural pubs offering bar meals and beach kiosks where you can tuck into a crab sandwich.

FRUITS OF THE SEA

At its best, Guernsey fare draws on locally produced ingredients. Seafood features on virtually every menu. For a full blow out, order a Breton-style *plateau de fruits de mer*, and work your way through a king-size seafood banquet of oysters, scallops, crabs,

Above: freshly caught crab for sale at the fish market in St Peter Port.

mussels and lobster. The nicely plump chancre crab is the most widely available but the sweeter spider crab is more sought after. The catch of the day is likely to be chalked up on a board. Sea bass, bream, brill, grey mullet, monkfish, turbot, mackerel and sole still inhabit Guernsey waters.

With France a short hop away, it is not surprising that Gallic dishes appear on menus. There are good farmhouse cheeses from Normandy and fresh French baguettes can be bought from bakers in St Port (try, for example, Boulangerie Victor Hugo in Le Pollet). But generally speaking it is British cuisine that prevails. You won't have to go far to find a fry-up breakfast, Sunday roast or scampi and chips.

The national dish is Guernsey Bean Jar, a variation of the French cassoulet. This hearty dish, comprised of various kinds of dried beans, plus

Above: cream tea using milk from Guernsey cows in the clotted cream.

F Guernsey Ormer

If you are on the island between January and April, during spring tides, you may see locals in waterproofs and wellies wading out in search of the ormer shellfish. Related to the abalone, it is found beneath rocks on the island's tidal sandbanks, and has a distinctive shell, well camouflaged from the outside but beautifully irridescent inside with a pearly rainbow sheen. Once a staple of the Channel Islanders' diet, the numbers of molluscs have dwindled and nowadays there are stringent regulations to protect the stocks.

Above: the ormer is sometimes called the abalone or ear-shell.

pork, onions and herbs, is traditionally cooked overnight in a stone bean jar and served with crusty bread.

Market gardening thrives on the islands, but even Guernsey dwellers will bend the knee to the deliciously earthy new potatoes grown by rival Jersey and likely to be found on the menu from March onwards. Tomatoes, celery, courgettes, peppers and most other salad ingredients will be locally grown. Home-grown strawberries will be accompanied, as likely as not, by delicious Guernsey cream. This is sure to find its way into all sorts of dishes, from teatime scones and cream to soups and sauces, along with the bright yellow Guernsey butter that will be spread on a slice of traditional Guernsey *gâche* (fruit loaf, pronounced 'gosh').

Dining hours are the same as those in the UK at lunch time, but evening meals tend to be served earlier, especially at seaside restaurants where last orders are often at 8pm.

LOCAL BREWS

Randalls, established in St Peter Port in 1868, now have a state-of-the-art brewery on St George's Esplanade.

Guided tours (Saturdays at 11am Apr–Sept, bookings essential, tel: 01481-720 134) show how water, malt hops and yeast are converted into Breda Lager and Patois Real Ale, then visitors are treated to a free post-tour pint. The only island to produce wine is Sark, which has 27 acres (11 hectares) of newly-planted vineyards. An expert Bordeaux winemaker and consultant studied the soil and meteorological data for months before choosing the best spot and the most suitable grape varieties. Decent quality white and reds should be available from 2014, with fizz to follow.

Find our recommended restaurants at the end of each Tour. Below is a price guide to help you make your choice.

Eating Out Price Guide

Two-course meal for one person, including a glass of wine.

£££	over £30
££	£20-30
£	under £20

Tour 1

St Peter Port

Explore on foot Guernsey's endearingly quaint capital, taking in the colourful port, old town and museums. Allow a whole day for this 3¾-mile (6km) walk

Hugging the slopes that rise steeply back from the sea, St Peter Port creates a spectacular vista as you arrive by sea. Church steeples and steep-roofed granite houses are stacked on the hillside while in the harbour below the forest of boat masts jostle for attention, lending the capital an almost Mediterranean air.

This is the oldest community in the Channel Islands, and it shows. The discovery of a Roman wreck in the harbour in 1985 indicated that this part of Guernsey's coastline was a refuge for seamen even in ancient times. The Town Church existed as early as 1048 and a castle has stood here since 1206, though today's town is made up mainly of finely preserved late Georgian and Regency buildings.

Highlights

- Castle Cornet
- La Vallette Underground Military Museum
- No. 26 Cornet Street
- Hauteville House
- Candie Gardens and Guernsey Museum

From the 12th to the 16th centuries fishing was the main activity, and St Peter Port was merely a small quayside settlement. It was through privateering that the town grew in size and wealth. In 1778 alone local privateers brought in £343,500 of booty. Wealthy merchants built fine houses and new buildings spread

Previous pages: lobster pots near Fermain Bay. **Left**: view from St Peter Port across to Castle Cornet.

up the slopes around the town and onto the plateau above. The granite houses appear piled on top of one another. The seafront Esplanades are lined by tall and unadorned warehouses, most converted to shops, pubs and restaurants. The grander houses of 18th-century merchants, on the hilltop above, have also undergone conversion – some of the fine houses along Grange Road and The Queen's Road now belong to wealthy banks and financial organisations, but their conversion has been carried out with sympathy for the original buildings.

THE WATERFRONT

A good place to begin exploring the town is the excellent **Guernsey Information Centre ❶** (tel: 01481-723 552; www.visitguernsey.com; Mon–Fri 9am–5pm, Sat 9am–1pm; also Sat pm and Sun am June–Sept), on North Esplanade, with its informative displays and helpful staff. The centre is housed in a building of 1911 whose grey granite makes it look rather austere – perhaps deliberately so, as this was once Guernsey's administrative centre, where all the departments needed to run the island were based. The information centre sits on land that was reclaimed at the beginning of the 20th century.

The centre organises interesting walks, with accredited guides, some

Above: walking down the Constitution Steps in St Peter Port.

departing from their office in St Peter Port. Themes include 'Ghosts, Graves and Famous Men', 'Smuggling' and 'On the Trail of Victor Hugo'. During the annual Spring and Autumn Walking Weeks an extensive programme on the island includes history, flora and fauna.

Originally ships docked right alongside the warehouses that line **Quayside**. This allowed cargoes of wine, citrus fruits, spices, sugar and wool to be lifted straight from the ship's hold into the tall Dutch-style warehouses, whose large loading doors have been replaced by windows. Most of them are four or five storeys tall, with one set of shops on the lower two floors, entered from Quayside, and another set of shops on the upper floors entered from the High Street. Linking Quayside and the High Street are a number of steep lanes, called *venelles* (Guernsey-French dialect for 'little passages'). Look up as you explore them – some are roofed over using massive timbers from broken-up ships.

THE HARBOUR

On the opposite side of Quayside is the **harbour ②**, with a mixture of yachts, cargo ships and inter-island

Above: the harbour of St Peter Port is still an active port for local fishermen, who provide the freshest catch to local restaurants.

Ⓕ Profiting from Piracy

From the late 18th century St Peter Port prospered from the practice of privateering. This was a form of legal piracy whereby ships were licensed by the British Government to capture enemy vessels and confiscate their cargoes. As England imposed duty on imported luxury goods as a means of funding its wars with France, Spain and the American colonies, Guernsey became a major supplier in the smuggling trade, shipping large quantities of captured brandy, perfume and lace to England.

Above: Guernsey's proximity to France made it an ideal hideaway for pirates.

ferries. With the advent of the steamship service between Guernsey and England, new facilities were called for; in 1853 the harbour area grew from 4 acres (1.6 hectares) to over 80 acres (32 hectares), with two long breakwaters installed 13 years later. Albert Pier and North Pier enclose the Old Harbour, where yachts are moored in the marinas.

The less picturesque St Julian's Pier to the north was added in the 1920s to make way for cargo ships and ferries. Today high-speed catamarans sail for mainland Britain and France. At the landward end of the pier you're unlikely to miss the Travel Trident booth selling tickets for ferries to Herm, the diminutive car-free island which you can see in the distance. Further along the pier you can purchase tickets for Sark, another popular day trip island, one step further to the southeast.

LIBERATION PLACE

Close to the Travel Trident booking kiosk, the **Liberation Monument** ❸, a granite 'needle', commemorates the liberation of Guernsey from Occupying German forces on 9 May 1945. It was here that crowds of is-

landers greeted the British liberators after five years under German rule. On Liberation Day each year, and only on this day, the monument casts a shadow onto the plaques on the adjacent granite bench, each marking a key

Above: the Liberation Monument was designed by Guernsey artist Eric Snell.

Above: a stroll along the breakwater makes for a pleasant evening.

event of that jubilant day. The monument is designed so that the tip of the shadow reaches each commemorative plaque at the precise time of the event it commemorates.

THE TOWN CHURCH

Heading south, you will come to St Peter Port's busiest road junction, overlooked by a **statue of Prince Albert**, erected to commemorate a visit made by Victoria and Albert in 1846. Opposite is the parish church of

Above: the bell tower of Town Church decorated with hanging baskets.

St Peter Port, or the **Town Church ❹**, whose sturdy steeple rises above the waterfront. Although it incorporates the nave of the town's earlier medieval church, much of the original fabric was damaged during the Civil War and the building underwent major restoration in the 19th century. One of the war's ironies was that the town, and the castle that was intended to protect it, were on opposite sides in the conflict. St Peter Port sided with the Parliamentarians, whilst the governor of Guernsey supported the Royalist cause and successfully survived a nine-year siege from his base in Castle Cornet. The Royalists bombarded the town with such success that shipping was forced to move to St Sampson's harbour, further up the coast. Note how close the Albion House Tavern is to the church, almost within touching distance. This is the closest inn to a church in the British Isles.

CASTLE CORNET

Built to protect the settlement in the 13th century, Guernsey's castle was formerly isolated on a rocky islet, and accessible only by boat. A breakwater and bridge were built in the 19th century and today's visitors explore the castle by walking out along the Victorian Castle Pier. (Be sure to get the right pier; from the Esplanade you can be fooled into thinking the castle lies

Above: looking down on Sutler's Garden at Castle Cornet.

at the end of the shorter Albert Pier.) A great breakwater stretches beyond the castle, with a lighthouse at the far end where optimistic anglers cast their lines. A third of the way along the pier you can divert left to **Fish Quay**, where the workaday fishing boats land their catch and gulls swoop down in the hope of tasty morsels. The fruits of the fishermen's labour, including live lobsters, can be seen and bought at Seafresh fishmonger on the pier. Continue along the pier to **Castle Cornet** ❺ (www.museums.gov.gg; Apr–Oct daily 10am–5pm, guided tours most days at 10.30am; charge), enjoying fine views of Havelet Bay and the town skyline. Shielding the entrance of St Peter Port harbour, this major monument is a delightful maze of buildings and courtyards, linked by steps and passageways, with little gardens tucked into sheltered corners. The castle was a stronghold of the English Crown for nearly 800 years, and now several buildings within the grounds have been converted into museums. Allow plenty of time if you want to see it all; try and time a visit to coincide with the **noonday gun ceremony**, when an 18th-century cannon is fired.

The oldest part of the castle survives only in fragmentary form – the original keep and most of the medieval buildings were destroyed when the castle magazine was struck by lightning on 29 December 1672, killing the governor's wife and mother, and five other people. Displays show the results of archaeological excavation to recover the form of the original medieval

ⓕ Castle Entertainment

On summer afternoons from Tuesday to Saturday the Living History performers present a series of stories about life in Castle Cornet and St Peter Port from Tudor times to the German Occupation. In July and August outdoor theatre in the castle grounds ranges from Shakespeare's *Comedy of Errors* to *James and the Giant Peach*. Look out too for Castle Nights in high season, offering free evenings of music and live entertainment from 6–9pm.

Above: historical performers provide summer entertainment at the castle.

castle, while the present fortress is substantially Tudor in date. It was the first English-built castle to incorporate ideas borrowed from Italy – thicker masonry to absorb cannon fire, as few vertical faces as possible (oblique and rounded faces were better at deflecting cannon balls) and bastions projecting at intervals along the curtain wall to provide gun platforms and protect from a direct attack.

The success of this design was proved during the Civil War siege, when the castle proved all but impregnable, and again when, during World War II, the Germans occupied the castle and found it necessary to make very few modifications to fit it for modern warfare.

The castle contains a number of interesting museums. The **Maritime Museum** in the Upper Barracks building examines the relationship between St Peter Port and the sea from Roman times through to today's high-speed catamarans.

The exhibits include displays from the Gallo-Roman wreck recovered from the harbour mouth in 1985, well-preserved pottery from medi-

eval wrecks and a gallery of marine art. **The Story of Castle Cornet**, housed in the Lower Barracks, traces 700 years of turbulent history, including an audio presentation on the explosion of 1672, which destroyed much of the early castle. The **201 Squadron RAF Museum** covers 'Guernsey's Own' air heroes. In the 18th-century hospital buildings the **Royal Guernsey Militia Museum** depicts the tragic story of the death of the Royal Guernsey Light Infantry in spring 1917; and the new **Royal Guernsey Light Infantry** tells the story of the regiment, which was formed during World War I and served in France.

In a spacious gallery in the Upper Barracks Building, and only open for specific events, is the lovely **Hatton Gallery**, full of portraits of past governors and well-known merchants, dramatic seascapes and some fine views of St Peter Port.

(A Discovery Pass, available from the Guernsey Information Centre, North Esplanade or at the museums allows unlimited entry to Castle Cornet, the Guernsey Museum and Fort Grey, with accompanying children going free).

Above: cannons defended the walls of Castle Cornet from invaders.

Above: the Underground Military Museum's collection of artefacts.

LA VALLETTE UNDERGROUND MILITARY MUSEUM

Continuing along South Esplanade you will come to the town's main bathing beach to your left (sandy at low tide) before reaching the green end of St Peter Port, where gardens and trees cloak the steep hill above the under-cliff footpath. Continue along here for a short way and you will soon reach **La Vallette Underground Military Museum** ❻ (www.la valette.tk; Mar–mid-Nov daily 10am–5pm; charge). The simple concrete-lined opening in the cliff leads into a complex of tunnels built by slave la-bourers during the Occupation. The tunnels served as a refuelling station for U-boats, and one of the huge fuel oil storage tanks has survived. The museum is packed with fascinating military and civilian memorabilia. The museum starts with a display of Red Cross food parcels delivered by the Swedish ship, the *Vega*, towards the end of the war, when the population of the Channel Islands was close to starving. To people used to surviving

❺ Occupation Tours

The Channel Islands were the only British territory to fall into German hands during World War II. The islands of Guernsey and Jersey were invaded in June 1940 and were turned into fortresses. In May 1945, after five long years, British forces liberated the islands. To find out more about the Occupation, and visit some of the German fortifica-tions, you can join an Occupation Tour run by Island Coachways (www.icw.gg; Thursday only).

Above: a temporary exhibit of art created during the Occupation.

on a meagre diet of seaweed jelly, bramble-leaf tea and parsnip-root coffee, the food parcels, filled with milk, cheese, butter, chocolate, oatmeal and peas, would have come as much-needed relief.

Right next to these displays, relating to the final difficult months of the war, are posters detailing arrangements for the evacuation of the islands in 1940, when it was clear that the Germans intended to invade. What was not clear, as the posters show, was whether or not the British government intended to send an evacuation ship to rescue those islanders who wished to leave. In the end, 9,000 people – more than half the islands' population – managed to escape in fishing boats and cargo steamers, including almost the entire population of Alderney.

Above: one of the tunnels at the Underground Military Museum.

Another exhibit reminds us that most of the islands' fortifications were constructed by forced labour – whips and rubber truncheons bring home the brutal nature of the Channel Islands' regime. The people were protected from exploitation, to a degree, by the Hague Convention, which the Germans observed, stating that local people could not be forced to construct works of military character, especially against their own country. Even so, there were reprisals against the civilian population, including the confiscation of radio sets, and executions for acts of so-called espionage. Others were interned in Biberach Camp, in Bavaria, from September 1942 until May 1945, and there are some moving exhibits of Christmas gifts and cards made by the internees and sent back to their families.

LA VALLETTE BATHING POOLS

Across the road from La Valette Underground Military Museum, the seafront promenade affords fine views of Castle Cornet and neighbouring islands. At low tide you can spot **La Vallette Bathing Pools**, public swimming pools since Victorian times. The first was the Horseshoe, built in 1859 with a small dressing room, then

Ⓢ VAT-Free Shopping

In theory, shopping in the Channel Islands ought to be cheap because there is no VAT to pay on purchases and because import duties are low. In reality, the cost of freighting goods to the islands often cancels out the gains. Before purchasing jewellery, cameras and electronic goods you should do your research and have a good idea how much the same item would cost back home.

Above: boutique shopping on Mansell Street, Old Town.

Above: there are 47 displays of marine life at the Guernsey Aquarium.

the Ladies and Gents in 1876 and the Children's pool added in 1896. Today all four pools – when they are not submerged by the tides – are open to all free of charge. This is the meeting place of the Guernsey Polar Bears Swim Group who swim all year round, regardless of the weather.

THE AQUARIUM

The South Esplanade continues a short way to another tunnel: this one was built in 1861, as part of a scheme, never completed, for building a road through to Fermain Bay *(see page 34)*. The Germans constructed several side tunnels, using Russian labourers who left their hammer and sickle symbol on the rocky roof.

Today the tunnels house the **Aquarium** ❼ (tel: 01481-723 301; Mon–Sat 10am–6pm, Sun 10am–5.30pm; charge), displaying examples of the many and varied fish to be found in Guernsey's waters – from perfectly camouflaged baby soles and the tiny inhabitants of tidal pools, to larger conger eels and dogfish. There are also prettily patterned tropical fish, with notes on their habitats and suitability for use in home aquariums, a collection of reptiles in a vivarium and a new terrapin island. Fish are fed two or three times a week on squid,

beef heart, sand eel and sprats; lizards are treated with fresh fruit and live insects such as crickets and locusts.

THE HIGH TOWN

Returning to Castle Pier, the causeway that leads out to Castle Cornet, climb up the steep lanes on the left that lead right past the Yacht Inn, turn left to the cobbled intersection of four alleys, then right up Coupée Lane. You should come out alongside **No. 26 Cornet Street** ❽ (Easter–Sept Tue–Sat 10am–4pm,) a remarkable building that serves as the headquarters of the National Trust of Guernsey. The offices lie behind the well-restored 18th-century shop and parlour, where volunteers in period costume sell gift and souvenirs, as

Above: an indigenous lobster at the Guernsey Aquarium.

Above: Hauteville House was personally decorated by Victor Hugo.

well as sweets, which are measured in pounds and ounces.

Turn left out of the shop, and you will pass, on the right, the former church of St Barnabas, the home of the Island Archives; from the car park there is a superb view over the red-tiled rooftops of Guernsey. Further along, Tower Steps, with its pubs and

Above: Victor Hugo spent 15 years living at Hauteville House.

restaurants, has a pleasing group of late Georgian and Regency buildings and beyond, on the right, lies Pedvin Street, with a long curving terrace of late Georgian houses.

Continue left here into **Hauteville**, where the increasingly large and ornamented houses and villas give some indication of the status and wealth of the people who first settled here when the area began to be developed in the 1780s.

HAUTEVILLE HOUSE

The street's most famous resident was Victor Hugo, the great French romantic poet, writer and politician. In 1856 he bought No. 38, **Hauteville House ❾** (tel: 01481 721 911; www.victorhugo.gg; guided tours by appointment only, in English or French, May–Sept Mon–Sat 10am–4pm, Apr noon–4pm; charge) and lived there for 15 years. The house has been preserved as it was and the gardens brought back to their original splendour. Hugo was more than a little eccentric, and the house is a physical manifestation of his quirky ideas about monarchy, history and patriarchy.

la mère de mes enfants') and family at Hauteville House, and Juliette Drouet, his mistress (*'Madame, mon amie'*) at No. 20 Hauteville, which had been his first Guernsey home. This was sufficiently close for Hugo to signal to his mistress from his bedroom window.

Whilst living here he wrote some of his best-selling novels, including *Les Misérables* and *Les Travailleurs de la Mer (The Toilers of the Sea)* which is set in and around Guernsey and demonstrates Hugo's intimate knowledge of the island. Growing wealthy for the first time, Hugo indulged his taste for woodworking and interior decoration. Thanks to the anti-Church zeal and anarchy of the Napoleonic period, churches throughout Europe had been gutted of woodwork and paintings, and antiques dealers had huge stocks of Renaissance and medieval carvings for sale.

Hugo bought chests and pews and broke them up to line the walls and ceilings of his rooms, adding his own embellishments, to create a house that is dark, brooding and full of symbolic meaning. Significantly, he chose to write his powerfully romantic novels in a room that was, by contrast with the rest of the house, flooded with light – he constructed a rooftop observatory of glass, with

Having been thrown out of France, branded as a dangerous radical for his opposition to the *coup d'état* staged by Prince Louis Napoléon in 1851, Hugo first settled in Jersey, where he kept up a tirade against *'Napoléon le petit'* as he styled the French emperor, through his newspaper, *L'Homme*. In the same paper, he criticised Queen Victoria for making a state visit to Paris in 1855. This so angered the people of Jersey that Hugo was expelled once again – this time moving a short distance north to the island of Guernsey. Here he installed his wife (*'Madame,*

Ⓕ Forever French

Despite living in the Channel Islands for 18 years, and feeling at home here, Victor Hugo never learned to speak English. *'When England wants to chat with me, let her learn my language'*. His heart always belonged to France, and one of the reasons he chose the Channel Islands when he was exiled from France was that his native language was understood.

Above: Victor Hugo and family in a group portrait session.

F Top of the Tower

For great views over St Peter Port, Sark and Herm, climb up the Victoria Tower built in 1846 in honour of a visit from Queen Victoria, the first reigning monarch to travel to the island. The tower is in Monument Gardens, close to the Guernsey Museum (*see p.28*), and the key must be collected from (and returned to) the museum.

far-reaching views over the blue seas to his beloved France. The family home was an open house to many eminent visitors during Hugo's lifetime. Despite its quirkiness Hauteville House is stately and grand. You can view the building only on a conducted tour, though the eminently knowledgeable guides make this one of the best places you can visit anywhere on the Channel Islands.

The gardens of Hauteville House have been faithfully renovated by the city of Paris, and include a kitchen garden, fruit trees and Hugo's United States of Europe Oak – a living link with this great visionary.

Above: Christie's cafe is ideal for breakfast, lunch or dinner.

Above: Market Square.

MARKET SQUARE AND TOWN CENTRE

From Hugo's house, turn left and explore Hauteville, then turn right down Park Lane Steps, just before the Marton Guest House. At the bottom of the stairway turn right to reach leafy Trinity Square. This corner of St Peter Port has a choice of restaurants and, on cobbled and pedestrianised Mansell Street which leads back to the centre of town, a number of shops.

You will emerge at **Market Square** ❿ where the old market has undergone a multimillion pound restoration and is now a 21st-century shopping mall. Much of the facade has been preserved and the square is a pleasant spot to sit and watch the world go by. Produce from across the island is brought to the weekly Fresh Friday market, while on Saturdays in summer the square is the venue for open-air concerts and drama.

Even if you aren't a keen shopper, it's worth exploring the maze of the Arcades, to the left as you emerge from Market Street, along with the High Street and its extension, **Le Pollet** ⓫ and Lower Pollet. Many of the shops along these streets have attractive Regency, Victorian and Edwardian shop fronts – and there are plenty of inviting cafés where you can stop for coffee or cakes.

CIVIC ST PETER PORT

At the junction of High Street and Le Pollet, Smith Street leads left and uphill towards the **Royal Court House**, centre of island government and administration. Walking up Smith Street, do not miss the lace-like detailing of the ironwork decorating the facade of Marks & Spencer and the estate agent next door.

At the top of the hill, to the left, is the sombre court house, in which the States of Deliberation, which governs the Bailiwick of Guernsey, held its first meetings in 1803. In the same building are the island's courts – civil and criminal. They are located only a short step away from Guernsey's main police station, which occupies the former workhouse, La Maison de Charité. To find it, turn round and go past the little garden at the top of Smith Street, then head straight across, down Hirzel Street. This will bring you to the gates of the former workhouse. On the gatehouse is a plaque showing a pelican pecking

her breast to feed her young with her own blood, the traditional symbol of charitable self-sacrifice, and the 1742 date stone.

Turn left here and walk up Hospital Lane to emerge on St Julian's Avenue. To the right is a **War Memorial** to Guernsey and Alderney officers and men killed in the Boer War; to the left, along College Street, is St James, a deconsecrated garrison church providing Guernsey with a versatile venue for concerts, drama, lectures and exhibitions. Part of the complex is the

Above: the facade of the Royal Court House.

Above: the historic Candie Gardens were established in 1894.

purpose-built Dorey Centre, housing the **Guernsey Tapestry** ⑫ (www. guernseytapestry.org.gg; Mon–Sat 10am–4pm; charge). The display comprises 10 separate tapestries, each one representing a century of Guernsey's history. These historically accurate and meticulously worked scenes were created by the 10 Guernsey parishes to mark the new millennium and each one bears the crest of the relevant parish. The stories in the panels are brought to life by an audioguide – you can also find out more by chatting to the volunteers who work here, many of whom helped stitch the tapestries.

Across the road lies the imposing Elizabeth College, founded in 1563, and named after Queen Elizabeth I, though the building you see today dates from 1829. Having crossed the road, turn right for the peaceful **Candie Gardens** ⑬ (all year until dusk) in Candie Road. Once part of a private estate, the gardens were bequeathed to the islanders in 1871 and turned into a public park. On sunny days locals and visitors stretch out on the lawn and admire the wonderful views. A pretty French-style cast-iron bandstand has been converted into an excellent café, where brass bands strike up on summer Sunday afternoons. The museum diplomatically separates a statue of Queen Victoria, installed in 1897, from a more flamboyant one of her critic, Victor Hugo, in the gardens.

GUERNSEY MUSEUM AND ART GALLERY

The **Guernsey Museum and Art Gallery** ⑭ (www.museums.gov.gg; daily 10am–4pm, Apr–Oct until 5pm;

Ⓚ Beau Séjour

Guernsey vies with Jersey for the highest sunshine totals in the British Isles. But rain can be a problem in springtime. This is the time to take the youngsters to the Beau Séjour Leisure Centre (www.beausejour. gg, open daily) on the hilltop above St Peter Port, to enjoy the swimming pool, with its flume slides and floating islands. You can go for the day or buy a family holiday pass for a week or fortnight entitling you to unlimited swimming, along with tennis, squash and badminton.

Above: Beau Séjour offers sports, musical events and comedy.

charge) is built around a collection left to the States of Guernsey by Thomas Guille and Frederick Allès, who emigrated to New York and became partners in an interior decorating business. As they prospered, they poured their wealth into books about the Channel Islands, which they eventually bequeathed, along with antiquities, weapons and furniture. Exhibits include finds excavated from local megaliths and tombs by F.C. Lukis, Guernsey's pioneering 19th-century archaeologist.

These are joined by informative exhibits on the geology, wildlife, and history of Guernsey.

Exhibits in the adjacent art gallery include Rodin's bust of Victor Hugo (1883), wearing a most expressive frown and wild beard and charracterful sketches by Peter de Lièvre (1812–78) of island farmers and fishermen, giving an insight into life on the island in Victorian times. For little ones there is a Discovery Room, activity box, puzzle sheets and traditional costumes.

Ⓔ Eating Out

Da Nello's
Le Pollett; tel: 01481-721 552; lunch and dinner.
The locals' favourite Italian restaurant with a covered courtyard, serving a wide range of traditional pasta, seafood and meat dishes. ££–£££

La Frégate
Les Cotils, St Peter Port, tel: 01481-724 624, lunch and dinner.
Outstanding slightly formal restaurant with magical views of the harbour and outer islands. International cuisine using local products wherever possible. Regarded by many as the best food on the island. £££

Hojo
Norman House, South Esplanade; tel: 01481-725 632; www.hojo.gg; Tue–Sat from 10am to late, Mon 10am–7pm.
New restaurant serving innovative Japanese cuisine in a relaxed setting. Think spicy miso soup with lobster or rib eye steak with garlic crisps and wafu sauce. Or make your own at sushi-rolling fun nights (£40 per head) when sake flows. ££–£££

Le Nautique
Quay Steps; tel: 01481-721 714; www.lenautiquerestaurant.co.uk; closed Sun, and Sat lunch.
One of the top seafood restaurants, with lovely views over the marina and an old-fashioned atmosphere. £££

The Old Quarter
15 Mansell Street; tel: 01481-727 268; closed Sun and dinner on Tue. Good value no-frills food with an Irish twist (Paddy is the genial chef). The three-course lunch or early dinner set menu is a bargain at £11.95. £–££

Le Petit Bistro
56 Le Pollet; tel: 01481-725 055; www.petitbistro.co.uk; closed Sun. Authentic French cuisine in atmospheric bistro. Specialities feature *coq au vin*, *coquille St Jacques* and frogs' legs. Excellent-value lunches and early-bird dinners. The adjoining Le Petit Café is open all day. £–££

Pier 17
Albert Pier; tel: 01481-720 823; www.pier17restaurant.com.
One of the island's most popular restaurants with a contemporary setting and great views over the working harbour and Castle Cornet. Book well in advance. ££–£££

RED
61, The Pollet; tel: 01481-700 299; www.red.gg; closed Sat lunch and Sun. A cool new grill house and cocktail bar where top quality cuts of beef (Porterhouse and rib on the bone among them) are cooked on a charcoal grill. Non-carnivores are catered for with roast or grilled market fish, and vegetarians with the likes of goat's cheese soufflé and asparagus and morel mushroom risotto. ££–£££

Fables & Festivals

Fairies, witches and superstition reign supreme in Guernsey, where people sometimes still look askance at the water lanes and ancient dolmens that dot the landscape.

According to Guernsey locals, the few remaining water lanes (where a rushing stream tumbles downhill beside the path) are the abode of fairies. Not the butterfly-like creatures that inhabit the pages of Arthur Rackham fairy tales, but Shakespeare's fairies – creatures that delight in wreaking havoc on human lives, turning the milk sour, preventing the cream from turning to butter or tripping the horse as it plods down the lane.

Tales abound on the islands of myth, superstition and strange custom. The prehistoric menhirs and dol-

mens gave rise to devil worship and witchcraft. In Guernsey witches were said to meet at Le Catioroc, where they rubbed *le verjus au diable* (a hallucinatory cream) on their bodies and shouted across the sea to the small priory of Lihou '*Tcheit d'la Haout, Marie d'Lihaou*' ('Fall from up there, Mary of Lihou'). From 1550–1661 more than 170 Channel Island 'witches' were tried. At a notorious witchcraft trial in 1617 three Guernsey women were accused of killing both islanders and cattle by practising witchcraft. They were tortured to elicit a confession, convicted, tied to a stake, strangled from behind and burnt. Some islanders are still superstitious.

The islands have a host of annual festivals and events, ranging from local events such as the Torteval Scarecrow Festival to big crowd-pullers such as the August Battle of Flowers where locals compete to win the Prix D'Honneur for the best floral float. Alderney may be associated with grim

Above: festival-goers at Le Viaer Marchi honour historical food and dress.
Left: re-enactors dress in military garb for Liberation Day, when the island celebrates the end of German Occupation.

Occupation-era fortifications, but it has some of the best festivals on the Channel Islands. If you happen to be there on the first Sunday in May, between noon and 2pm, you'll be hailed with a free Milk o' Punch at any of the island's pubs. The punch is made from milk and egg, with a healthy tot of rum and some mystery ingredients. However, the island's biggest draw is Alderney Week, when 3,000 visitors descend on the island for a man-powered flight competition (with competitors launching themselves off the harbour at Braye with their home-made 'planes'); a daft raft race around the bay; duck races and other fun events for all ages.

Tour 2

St Peter Port to Moulin Huet Bay

Walk along flower-clad cliffs, dip down to beautiful bays and enjoy spectacular sea views. An exhilarating walk of 7½ miles (12km) which takes five hours, allowing for breathers

Allow a whole day for this coastal walk, taking a picnic lunch or stopping for freshly caught seafood. Fermain Bay with its café/restaurant makes an ideal place for a break. Parts of the walk are quite steep, particularly as the path climbs up from the bays, but there is nothing that would challenge an averagely fit adult, and the paths are in good condition. Public buses Nos 81, 91 or 11 can provide transport for part of the way. Timetables can be picked up at the Guernsey Information Visitor Centre, at the bus terminus or are available online at www.hctgroup.org. If you have a car, parking is available at both ends of the walk, at La Vallette (where you

> ## Highlights
> • Clarence Battery
> • Fermain Bay
> • Jerbourg Point
> • Petit Port
> • Moulin Huet Bay
> • Doyle Monument

will need a parking disc), and at Moulin Huet Bay. Although the footpath is well signed and fairly obvious, a map is nevertheless useful. The best map is the Ordnance Survey-style map of the Bailiwick of Guernsey (1:100,000) or alternatively *Perry's Official Channel*

Island Guide to Guernsey, a booklet with detailed maps, available from the tourist office. Remember to take binoculars for the birdlife, along with suncream, a hat and plenty of water.

ST PETER PORT TO FERMAIN BAY

Start from the South Esplanade in St Peter Port, and follow the roadside footpath past the open-air swimming pools (covered at high tide) and La Vallette Underground Military Museum, as far as the entrance to the Aquarium *(see page 23)* within the tunnel. Follow the steps up the cliff face to the left of the museum. Catch your breath by admiring the views from **Clarence Battery ❶** whose entrance is found near the top of the path *(see box, page 35)*. This headland is covered in Napoleonic-era fortifications.

From the battery, continue uphill. The path to the left drops down to **Soldier's Bay**, so-called because it was reserved for the soldiers from Fort George who used to come and swim here. Sadly this sheltered shingle and sand beach, which is good for swimming, has become impassable, and there is no public access.

FORT GEORGE

To the right and ahead as you climb the hill are some of the walls of **Fort George ❷**. This massive Georgian fort was built to house Guernsey's main garrison and to take over from Castle Cornet *(see page 18)* as the island's main stronghold, overlooking the approaches to St Peter Port. It served its purpose throughout the 19th century, then during World War II it became the headquarters of the Luftwaffe radar defences. An obvious target for Allied air raids the fort was severely damaged in the war. In the 1960s the site was sold to a private developer and the granite walls

Left: the view over Fermain Bay.
Above: the Clarence Battery.

now protect an up-market housing estate. The fort still retains an imposing gatehouse, with its 1812 date and the name of Sir John Doyle *(see Doyle Monument, page 39)*.

Turn left when you meet the tarmac road called La Corniche to follow the clifftop road for 400yds/metres, past balconied houses on Guernsey's largest open-market estate – a cross between the south of France and Los Angeles.

Where La Corniche bends to the right, the cliff path continues left, with fine views back to Soldier's Bay. Further fortifications line the path to the right as you climb away from the cliffs through woodland. At the next path junction, go left to descend through woods that are a haze of bluebells in the spring. At the next junction turn left to climb up to the clifftop again. As you follow the cliff path you will pass the 88 **Ozanne Steps** ❸ which were built by a former governor of Guernsey to provide access to a rock platform where he and his wife could bathe in privacy. Nowadays anyone can come and take a dip here.

FERMAIN BAY

Continue along the path until you come to a junction, then go straight

Above: looking down on Fermain Bay from a coastal pathway.

ahead, up the concrete steps, and turn left to follow a tarmac path which rounds the cliffs to give breathtaking views over **Fermain Bay** ❹, one of Guernsey's prettiest beaches. Bobbing with boats and washed by gentle waves, the bay has the air of the Mediterranean. This is a lovely spot for sunbathing, swimming in the clear waters (though sand is only exposed at low tide) and diving from the steps. Despite being one of Guernsey's most picturesque spots, the bay is rarely crowded since the only vehicular access is by a private road, closed to all but permit holders, and there is no nearby parking. This does not put off the punters coming by day or evening to the Fermain Beach Café, one of Guernsey's top café/restaurants and an ideal spot for a break. Beyond the café the round tower was one of 15 built along the coast in 1778–9 as defence against French attacks. Twelve of these towers still stand.

If you feel you have walked far enough, you could always head up the valley behind the bay to reach Fort Road and wait for one of the buses that pass at regular intervals. Alternatively, you can walk back to St Peter Port via Fort George Military Cemetery and Belvedere House.

FERMAIN BAY TO JERBOURG POINT

Leaving Fermain Bay by the bridge at the western end, follow signs for St Martin's Point. The path takes you through a forest of Monterey pines and affords fine views of the tiny island of Herm. Shortly after joining a road go left down a 'private drive' which is a right of way to the cliff path.

You can take a diversion down the valley to Marble Bay, named after the quartz found there, or turn immediately right towards the Jerbourg Road. The path takes you just above

Above: twitchers should head for the bird-hide at Jerbourg Point.

a seductive and secluded little sandy beach called **La Divette**, with a late medieval jetty. Continue along the heavily indented steep cliffs towards the exposed St Martin's Point.

JERBOURG POINT

A steep stepped climb brings you to the car park on **Jerbourg Point** ❺ where you'll also find toilets and a refreshment kiosk. To the left of the car park, the roof of the German Naval Battery Command Bunker provides a good lookout point for views of other Channel Islands. With good visibility you can see Jersey and the coast of France on the horizon as well as Alderney, Herm and Sark. Closer to, there are fine views of Vau Bêtes lying between St Martin's Point and Jerbourg. This is better known as **Telegraph Bay**, named after an old submarine telephone cable which used to be linked to Jersey.

Follow the road between the hotel and clifftop. Where the road bends to the right, just beyond a granite memorial to Bill Green, look for a path that leads off to the left. This goes down towards a German bunker – one of several along this route, all sited to take advantage of the panoramic views. The second bunker you pass is now used as a **birdwatching hide**, and maintained by the Royal Society for the Protection of Birds. From here you can (with binoculars)

Ⓥ Clarence Battery

Dating from 1782 Clarence Battery formed part of Fort George, built to defend St Peter Port from the threat of French invasion. Little remains of the battery but the ramparts have been restored and there are informative panels on the history of the structure. Stunning sea views take in St Peter Port and neighbouring Channel Islands. Nearest is Herm, and on a clear day you should also be able to see Sark and Alderney.

Above: Clarence Battery overlooks the sea, with Herm in the distance.

watch nesting gulls and shags on the nearby rock stacks, and linnets and whitethroats feeding among the cliff-top vegetation.

TOWARDS PETIT PORT

Continue along the path and eventually you will reach a memorial to Sir Victor Gosselin, in whose memory the nearby land was donated to the island of Guernsey. Straight ahead there are views of Moulin Huet Bay, which you now approach, continuing down the cliff path. Turn left where the cliff path joins a tarmac path, then left again after 20yds/metres, and left again shortly after. Keep taking the left turn each time a junction appears, passing several German bunkers. Over to the right you will see the obelisk of the Doyle Monument, which you will reach later, at the end of the walk.

The cliff path next meets a concrete path – turn left here and follow it down to a junction. The path to

the left goes down to **Petit Port** ❻ which – if you don't mind the long haul back up 300 steps – is a delightful bay and spot for bathing when the tide rolls out to reveal sand. Our route goes right along the cliff and left at the next junction. The path reaches some steps and comes out onto a tarmac road: go left and downhill to rejoin the cliff path, past a small spring and stream whose waters add lushness to the wooded valley. On the left, the granite wall of **Le Vallon estate** has strategically placed railings, allowing you a view of the ponds and fine gardens beyond the wall.

THE PEA STACKS

As you return to the clifftop, you are greeted by a superb view of the six rock formations known as **Les Tas de Pois d'Amont** ❼ (The Pea Stacks of the East). The rocks look like monks, with stooped backs and deep pointed hoods – especially the middle stack, which is known as Le

Above: walking down a meandering coastal footpath near Petit Port.

Above: a coastal view of the mis-named Pea Stacks and Jerbourg Point.

Petit Bonhomme d'Andriou (The Little Good Man Andrew). The story goes that Andriou, a pagan priest, witnessed a ship heading for the rocks in a storm and prayed to his gods to calm the waves. The weather only worsened so he then beseeched the Christian God, vowing to become a Christian if his prayers were answered. The ship was saved, Andriou was baptised and built a chapel on the site. In bygone days sailors used to pay

ⓕ Wildlife

The variety of colour, on clifftop path verges and in wooded valleys, creates a strong visual impact and shows what we have lost elsewhere through excessive use of herbicides. May is especially colourful, with red and white campion, the purples of massed thrift, the woodland bluebells and wild garlic. Don't forget to bring binoculars to spot fulmars, cormorants, shags – and the gannets and puffins that nest on offshore islets. Dolphins, grey seals and basking sharks are also occasionally spotted from the cliff paths.

Above: bluebells flower each spring in April and May.

Ⓕ South Coast Cliff Path

This delightful stretch of coastline may tempt the energetic to tackle the whole south coast cliff path. It is 15 miles (24km) from St Peter Port all the way to Pleinmont Headland in the west. The path requires a good deal of stamina, especially for the steep climbs up and down from the bays, and it's best to break it up. The walk can be done at any time of year, but the scenery is at its best in spring when wild flowers carpet the cliffs.

Above: rough steps have been hewn into the cliff.

their respects as they sailed past Andriou. Today the stacks are a habitat for nesting birds.

MOULIN HUET BAY

The path now passes through holm-oak woodland and eventually emerges at a tarmac road, by a pink and white farmhouse. The path to the left descends to the picturesque **Moulin Huet Bay** ❽ with its tea garden and striking rock formations. The bay was named after Monsieur Huet who owned a water mill *(moulin)* above the bay. The French Impressionist painter, Pierre-Auguste Renoir, was captivated by the bay's rock pools, cliffs and sea caves: he painted no fewer than 15 pictures of the scenic cove on a painting trip to Guernsey in 1883.

MOULIN HUET WINDMILL

No less scenic is the pretty lane to the right, the original site of the Moulin Huet windmill. If you walk up the lane, you can enjoy the sounds of gurgling water from a stream that

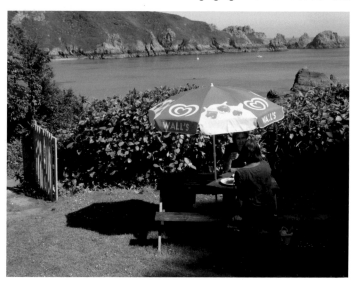

Above: the view across the bay from the tearoom at Moulin Huet Bay.

Above: distinctive rock formations can be seen at Moulin Huet Bay.

banks (according to Guernsey folk-legends lanes like this are the abode of fairies).

All too soon the path ends at a granite shelter that protects the spring. Alongside is a fine group of 17th-century farmhouses, one with a good example of a five-stone Guernsey arch over the front door. Here you should turn right to take the narrow path signposted Route Fainel, which passes between the farms. The lane emerges at a pretty **parish pump**, dated 1828, and a delightful neo-Gothic house whose wooden front doors are carved with windblown palm trees.

Turn left by the house to emerge onto a road. Turn right along the road, and left at the next junction. After a short distance you will meet the main Route de Jerbourg road. Turn right here to follow this road south.

is channelled along the right-hand side of the road.

Our route back lies up the even prettier **water lane** that leads off from the right-hand side of the car park, with another gurgling stream running in a stone-lined channel to the left. The path climbs steeply and narrows until there is just room to pass between steep, moss-covered

THE DOYLE MONUMENT

A short way beyond the pub, climb the mound up to the **Doyle Monument** ❾ for far-reaching views out to the Normandy coast. Named after Sir John Doyle, lieutenant-governor of Guernsey from 1803–16, this soaring granite column is a post-war replacement of the original, which the Germans demolished to prevent its use

---

⑮ French Spice

On a clear day you can see the French coast from Jerbourg Point. Geographically the Channel Islands belong naturally to France rather than to England and, not surprisingly, they have a heady mix of French and British cultures. The great French Impressionist, Pierre-Auguste Renoir, who appraised Guernsey's light with a painter's eye at Moulin Huet Bay, noticed

how 'the Anglo-Saxon miss sheds her prudery when she arrives in Guernsey'. Victor Hugo, for his part, was prepared to broaden her mind still further: ignoring Anglo-Saxon decencies altogether, he lived on the island with both wife and mistress, introducing them respectively as '*Madame, la mère de mes enfants*' and '*Madame, mon amie*'.

Above: Doyle Monument.
Right: Sausmarez Manor.

as a clandestine signal station. It was under Doyle's supervision that the modern road network on Guernsey was established – principally to allow for rapid troop movements at a time of continuing hostilities from France. Doyle also directed the building of Fort George, and was responsible for three Martello towers – Fort Grey, Fort Saumarez and Fort Hommet, which were built after a number of smaller towers erected more than 20 years earlier were deemed too small. The peninsula here had been fortified long before Doyle's arrival on the scene. You can still make out the three parallel lines of ramparts and trenches running to the cliff edge to either side of the monument. These were originally thought to be Roman but are in fact part of an even older Iron Age fortification. The stonewalling west of the monument is the only remnant of the Château de Jerbourg, a medieval castle mentioned in ancient documents.

Ⓔ Eating Out

Fermain Bay
Fermain Beach Café
Tel: 01481-238 636; lunch daily, dinner daily in high season.
This seafood café-cum-bistro is a great place to refuel after a bracing walk along the coast. Choose from crab sandwiches, scallops, seabass or surf and turf, and enjoy the views of this lovely bay. The secluded location entails a steepish walk down the hill – but it is well worth it. You need to book at least two weeks in advance for evening meals. £–££
Valley Restaurant
Fermain Valley Hotel, St Peter Port; tel: 01481-235 666; www.fermain valley.com; daily for breakfast, lunch, tea and dinner.
Contemporary brasserie in a swishly modernised hotel with fine views

from tiered terraces down to Fermain Bay. ££
Vintage Bella Tearooms
Moulin Huet; tel: 01481-238 636; daily 10am–6pm
Irresistible seaview tea gardens just up from the Moulin Huet Bay. A plaque on the path below the café indicates the spot where Renoir painted the bay. £

Jerbourg
The Auberge
Jerbourg, St Martins; tel: 01481-238 485; www.theauberge.gg; closed Sun dinner.
Consistently excellent food in a modern, minimalistic setting with stunning views. Head Chef Daniel Green, who trained at Harrods, draws inspiration from locally sourced produce. ££–£££

Tour 3

Southern Guernsey

A fine old manor house, historic museums and enticing bays with sparkling water make up this 26-mile (42km) day tour of southern Guernsey

To explore southern Guernsey, leave St Peter Port along the South Esplanade, passing Castle Cornet, then bear right to follow the main road uphill. The road twists up a delightful wooded valley to emerge on the grassy common that fronts the entrance to Fort George, the massive garrison that was built to protect St Peter Port at the turn of the 18th century. Turn left to follow Fort Road, and you will pass the Fermain Valley Hotel en route to the delightful Fermain Bay *(see page 34)*.

SAUSMAREZ MANOR

A little further along the main road, surrounded by gardens, lies **Sausmarez Manor ①** (daily 10am–5pm, www.sausmarezmanor.co.uk, grounds

(see page 34)

Highlights

- Sausmarez Manor
- Moulin Huet Bay
- Gran'mère de Chimquière
- Petit Bôt Bay
- German Occupation Museum
- Fort Grey

free apart from Artparks). Take a tour of the house (June–Sept Mon–Thur 10.30am, 11.30am and 2.30pm, first half Apr and second half of Oct Mon–Thur 11am, late Apr, May and first half of Oct Mon–Thur 10.30am and 11.30am; charge) and you will discover that this is the stronghold of one of Guernsey's oldest families: the de Sausmarez family have lived here

Above: the Sausmarez sculpture park offers a great variety of works.

since 1254, and a fine series of family portraits hangs in the imposing grey granite house, which dates from 1714. The family has been one of Guernsey's most distinguished dynasties for centuries, having served as bailiffs, governors, naval officers and diplomats. The refreshing lack of austerity is due to the fact that the manor is still lived-in. You may well come across the seigneur, Peter de Sausmarez, chatting to visitors. He also takes the Ghost Tours on Thursday evenings.

Only a fragment of the ancient building, in the form of an outhouse containing stonework, dates from the mid-13th century. Since then the manor house has been added to many times. Its most distinguishing feature is the Queen Anne facade, which was erected between 1714 and 1718, and replaced an earlier Tudor building. It was a refusal on the part of Sir Havilland de Sausmarez to modernise that saved much of this heritage from the Nazis. In 1940 the Germans were in-

tending to use Sausmarez Manor as a hospital but decided not to go ahead with their plans because the house did not yet have electric lighting.

MANOR GARDENS

Delightfully informal gardens surround the house, where you might possibly trip over free-range ducks and hens scrabbling for food in the undergrowth as you explore the lake and extensive woodlands. Unusually, overall admission is free, you just pay for the individual attractions. These include a nine-hole testing **pitch-and-putt course** (Apr–Dec daily 10am–5pm; equipment free with a deposit); the **Coppersmiths' Workshop** in the Tudor Barn where the craftsman is the only surviving coppersmith to make the Guernsey milk cans, used for centuries; **ride-on 7¼-gauge trains** for children's rides in the garden; a gift shop and a tearoom in the old vinery by the lakeside; and Le Petit Monde outlet with local products, souvenirs and ethically sourced home furnishings. Whether you're into art or not, don't miss **ArtParks**, one of the largest and most varied sculpture parks in Britain, set amid subtropical woodland. Showing around 220 works by 90 artists, this is a fascinating collection, from life-size figures to flying frogs, with a surprise

F Guernsey *Gâche*

Guernsey *gâche* (pronounced 'gosh') is one of the tastiest sweets of the Channel Islands, and consists of flour, butter, eggs, candied peel, sultanas, milk and sugar. Guernsey *gâche* in Jersey tastes different from Guernsey *gâche* in Guernsey. This is because each island jealously protects the purity of its own distinctive breed of cattle, which means that the milk of each island tastes slightly different.

Above: Guernsey *gâche* tastes best with a thick dollop of Guernsey butter.

round every corner. All of the exhibits are for sale, and have their prices alongside – but deep pockets are definitely required.

If you happen to be at Sausmarez Manor on a Saturday you're in for a treat. The **Farmers' Market** is held in the grounds from 9am–12.45pm and has a wonderful range of local produce: chancre and spider crabs, local beef and pork, free-range eggs, cheeses, Guernsey *gâche* and homemade cakes and pies. You will also find handmade arts and crafts, bric-a-brac, jewellery, antiques and plants.

From Sausmarez Manor turn right onto the main road, then straight on following the signs for Moulin Huet Bay. A left turn at the Bella Luce Hotel will take you down a pretty green lane from where there is a pleasant walk down to **Moulin Huet Bay ❷** with its sea caves and a waterfall. The bay is best enjoyed when the water is at half-tide or below, as the loveliest bits are covered by water at high tide. This is gorgeous landscape that inspired the paintings of Pierre-August Renoir.

LA GRAN'MÈRE DE CHIMQUIÈRE

Return to the main road, which brings you to **St Martin's Village**, with a cluster of shops and banks. It is worth finding a parking space in the centre and walking up the lane that leads northwards to visit St Martin's parish church and pay your respects to the

Gran'mère de Chimquière ❸.
This Grandma is considerably older
than most and, though stony faced,
she nevertheless flaunts her naked
breasts. She is, in fact, a 4,500-year-
old goddess carved in granite, standing
at the entrance to St Martin's churchyard and, if you visit after a wedding,
she is quite likely to be wearing a gar-
land of flowers: newlyweds traditionally place flowers on her head for luck.
Grandma was carved at two separate
stages: around 2,500BC the block of
granite was erected here, dressed and
smoothed to create a female figure
with breasts, folded arms and a gir-
dle. During late Roman times, around
AD200 or 300, the facial features were
recarved, and Grandma was given a
set of curls and a short buttoned cape
falling around her upper torso. The
crack through the torso is believed to
have been from an attack by a church
warden who was angry about the
worshipping of stone idols.

From St Martin's, follow signs to
the airport along Guernsey's south

Above: bathers enjoy the warmth of
the sun at Petit Bôt Bay.

coast road. To the left, after a mile
or so, some of the island's most attractive water lanes run down to
Petit Bôt Bay ❹, a small but popular bathing spot, especially when the
tide is out, and one of the island's
sunniest and most sheltered bays.
To reach it by car turn left after the

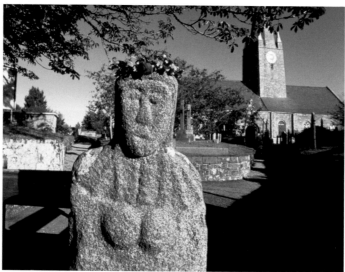

Above: Gran'mère de Chimquière is an ancient pagan goddess.

Deer Hound Inn. A Napoleonic-era tower stands guard over the bay, and what was once an old mill is now occupied by a tearoom. It is here that the best-known water lanes are to be found. The brooks that run down the sides of these lush green lanes used to power two mills, one of which was used for paper-making. The few remaining water lanes give a feel of how Guernsey used to be before the Occupation, when German forces surfaced over most of the streams.

GERMAN OCCUPATION MUSEUM

The next left turn off the main road leads to **Forest Church,** thought to have been built on the site of a dolmen, and then to the **German Occupation Museum** ❺ (daily 10am– 5pm, last admission 4pm; charge) which lies behind the church. This is an excellent war museum whose owner sells the tickets and makes the home-made cakes served in a pretty tea garden. Interesting and unusual items are displayed amongst the general mass of weapons, ration books, uniforms and medals. At the entrance are wartime photographs taken by German soldiers, in which they are cooking rabbit stew in a cauldron. A large painting depicts a Rhine Valley scene, complete with castle and vineyards, painted on the walls of a nearby house by a homesick soldier. Another rarity is a stone painted with a red V (for Victory) sign. Guernsey people showed their defiance by painting such signs wherever they could until the occupying troops took to painting laurel wreaths underneath to represent German victory.

There are some wartime condoms (German issue), a doll's house made from cardboard boxes, and letters from the Controlling Committee of the States of Guernsey giving instruc-

Ⓕ Haunted House

At Pleinmont Point, on the dramatic headland, a watchtower and an ex-military post is known as 'Victor Hugo's haunted house', having been immortalised by the writer in his novel of 1866, *Les Travailleurs de la Mer (The Toilers of the Sea)* which is set in Guernsey. The building was last used during World War I as a signalling station, but was then destroyed by the Germans in World War II, and today it lies in a state of ruin.

tions for the distribution of food during the dark days towards the end of the war when food was desperately short. Surprisingly, cigarettes did not need to be rationed – experiments in growing tobacco on Guernsey proved very successful, ensuring an unlimited supply of locally made cigarettes.

The museum's reconstruction of a wartime kitchen on Guernsey brings home just how little the islanders, and the occupying troops, had to live on, once the Allied landings in Normandy had cut off vital supply lines from

Above: the German Occupation Museum holds the finest collection of wartime effects in the Channel Islands.

Above: the Table des Pions, linked with fairies, witches and elves in local folklore.

the Continent. Surviving on a diet of bramble-leaf tea, acorn coffee, marrow pudding and potato bread, the only variety in the diet came from the occasional jelly made from carrageen moss (a type of seaweed) served with sugar beet syrup. There is also a reconstruction of a Guernsey street, with shops and people, as it looked in 1940, and there are videos explaining the various types of German fortifications to be seen around the island.

PLEINMONT PENINSULA

To see one of the most striking of these German fortifications, return to the main road and turn left at the junction. After about 3 miles (5km) you will pass **Torteval Church** on the right, with its distinctive round tower and witch's-hat spire. In a mile (1½ km) turn left, and head for the restored **Pleinmont Observation Tower** ❻ (Apr–Oct Wed–Sun 2–5pm, last admission 4.30pm; charge) with a car park nearby. A prominent feature on this windy headland, this is a five-storey concrete tower, pierced by viewing slots. It was from here that German observers controlled Guernsey's

coastal artillery, communicating with the gunners by radio.

On the same headland to the north is the **Table des Pions** ❼ also known as 'The Fairy Ring', a grassy mound encircled by a ditch. This spot played a prominent role in a medieval ceremony, the *Chevauchée de St Michel*, when officers of the feudal court in-

Above: a Celtic cross at Torteval Church memorialises war casualties.

spected the highways and sea defences to ensure that local landowners were fulfilling their duty to maintain them. The *pions* were the footmen who accompanied the officers and the Table des Pions was the spot where they took a break to enjoy an open-air banquet. The Chevauchée (briefly revived in 1995) was banned in 1837 because the *pions*, following what they claimed as an ancient right to kiss any women whose path they crossed, made free with the governor's wife.

Returning up Guernsey's western coast, there is a sheltered sandy beach at **Portelet Harbour**, lying at the foot of the dramatic south coast cliffs. This quiet cove with a small working harbour is a good spot for a swim if the tide is out. Beyond is a pretty wooded valley, owned by the National Trust of Guernsey.

ROCQUAINE BAY

Rocquaine Bay merges with **L'Erée Bay**, at low tide, to form one continuous stretch of sand – Guernsey's biggest beach, with safe swimming and rock pools to explore. In late July

Above: Rocquaine Bay has a long sandy beach at low tide.

the beach is the main focus of the Rocquaine Regatta, a full (and free) day and evening of entertainment and whacky events like raft racing.

FORT GREY

At the southern end of the bay you will find **Fort Grey** ❽ (Apr–Oct daily 10am–5pm; charge), named af-

ⓥ Guernsey on Foot

In the second week of June keen hikers join the 40-mile Itex charity walk (www.itexwalk.gg) around the coast of Guernsey. Participants can expect to complete the course in anything between 11–14 hours. Those who prefer shorter strolls can pick up a free walking map from the Guernsey Information Centre with details of coastal and inland walks plus all the attractions en route. Guernsey and its sister islands boast a rich variety of habitats for wildlife and birdlife; RSPB walks and events are organised throughout the year (www.rspb-guernsey.co.uk).

Above: explore Guernsey on a self-guided or organised walk.

ter the governor of the day, and built in 1804 as part of Sir John Doyle's grand scheme for defending Guernsey against potential attack from Napoleon's army. With its outer curtain wall and inner tower, the fort is aptly known as the Cup and Saucer. Today the tower is home to Guernsey's excellent **Shipwreck Museum**. The island's western shores, including the notorious Hanois reef, have seen numerous vessels come to grief. The sea surrounding Guernsey was for a long time the cornerstone of two important sea routes: the transatlantic run to the United States and the southerly run from Britain and northern Europe to the Mediterranean. Most disasters occurred in the peak shipping years of the 19th century. Building a lighthouse on the Hanois reef in 1862 reduced the annual toll of shipwrecks, and in 1975 the ship-

ping lane for ocean-going vessels was moved 10 miles (16km) west to avoid further casualties. The lower level of the museum features a whole range of finds from a ship's bell salvaged from the sea to cutlery and a fine candelabra, and coffee pots from SS *Yorouba*, which foundered in 1888.

During summer months the History in Action Company puts on performances at the fort in which the Militiaman recounts tales of derring-do.

If you're in need of refreshment cross the road to **Guernsey Pearl** ❾ (Mar–Oct daily 9.30am–5pm) which has a café serving an excellent crab salad and cream teas, with a sea-view terrace. Rather than being locally sourced, the pearls nearly all originate from the Far East, but are made up here; you can watch the art of pearl stringing in the workshop and purchase jewellery from the large showroom.

Above: Fort Grey is known to locals as the 'Cup and Saucer', due to its shape.

A GUERNSEY TO WEAR

Next door you can find items handmade by local craftsmen and artists, and Guernsey sweaters can be purchased from Le Tricoteur. While the word 'jersey' has entered the English language, the stylish Guernsey is far less well known, and the Alderney is a garment whose existence is known only to a few connoisseurs and knitwear historians (except in Australia, where the term is used for football shirts). The Guernsey sweater was originally made for seamen, the tightly knitted stitches producing a hardwearing garment. By the 19th century the Guernsey had become well known and Nelson adopted it as standard issue for the English navy.

SILBE NATURE RESERVE

Return to St Peter Port by taking the road inland, just north of Guernsey Pearl. Bird-lovers should seek out the **Silbe Nature Reserve** in the Rue

Above: the hard twist given to the dense wool fibres make the Guernsey sweater (originally made for fishermen) resistant to seaspray.

du Quanteraine, just to the north of the main road. Though it consists of little more than a group of fields watered by a stream in the Quanteraine Valley, it attracts plenty of birds, and is a pleasant spot for a stroll.

The main road brings you to St Peter's Parish Church, which sits on the side of a valley. A church has stood here since 1030, though the building you see today dates from the 14th and 15th centuries.

To return to St Peter Port take a right turn shortly after the church, which will take you past the airport, and back into town.

Eating Out

La Barbarie Hotel
Saint's Road, St Martin; tel: 01481-235 217; www.labarbariehotel.com; lunch and dinner.
Traditional bar food or an exotic seafood platter can be enjoyed by the pool of this old, country hotel. Four-course set dinners change daily. ££

Bella Luce Hotel
La Fosse, St Martin's; tel: 01481-238 764; www.bellalucehotel.com; lunch and dinner.
This is a stylish hotel in the peaceful green lanes of St Martin's, where you can come for light bar meals, a leisurely Sunday lunch or gourmet three-course dinners. Cuisine is contemporary and can be enjoyed either in the bar or the colonial-style dining room, which opens out onto a lovely walled garden for summer meals. ££

Café l'Escalier
Le Gouffre, Forest, tel: 01481-264 121; www.lescalierguernsey.co.uk;

daily 9am–late.
Lovely clifftop café/restaurant serving breakfast, lunch, cream teas and casual evening meals. A perfect spot for clifftop walkers in need of a respite. Paella is served outside on the seaview terrace on Sundays in summer. £–££

Deer Hound Inn
Le Bourg, Forest; tel: 01481-238 585; Mon–Sat 11am–late, Sun noon–late.
Good for pub grub and choice of beer and ales. Sunny terrace for meals alfresco, and Wi-fi. £

Water's Edge
Imperial Hotel, Pleinmont, Torteval; tel: 01481-264 044; lunch and dinner. Sea views towards Fort Grey are the big attraction here. You can come any time for bar meals, traditional cream teas or home-made cakes and coffee in the gardens. The à la carte menu features lobster and other seafood from the bay. £–£££

Shipwrecks

*'To be wrecked on the Casquets is to be cut into ribbons;
to strike on the Ortac is to be crushed into powder...'*
From *The Laughing Man (L'Homme qui Rit)* by Victor Hugo

When Alderney fisherman, Bertie Cosheril, pulled up a heavily encrusted musket with one of his lobster pots in 1984 he had little idea of the significance of his odd catch of the day. Further historical booty was discovered, but it was not until the early 1990s that archaeologists concluded that the items were coming from the wreck of *The Makeshift*, an English warship from the Elizabethan era. Over the years the sunken ship has yielded a treasure trove of artefacts. More than 1,000 items have so far been discovered, many of which have been preserved and are on display at the Alderney Society Museum.

DASHED UPON THE ROCKS

The treacherous rock-strewn coasts and strong currents around the Channel Islands have always posed a hazard for ships. From the earliest seafaring days two crucial trade routes passed close to Guernsey: from Britain and northern Europe to the Mediterranean and from the English Channel to America. But it was the 19th-century surge in trade that caused the largest number of shipping disasters. In bad weather captains would mistake the Channel Islands for the south coast of England and steer south, intending to head into the middle of the Channel but in fact aiming straight at the reefs.

Briseis, which struck a reef off Vazon Bay in 1947. The crew landed safely in lifeboats and, to the delight of the local people, a cargo of wine floated ashore. The Guernsey press reported 'amazing scenes of drunkenness, free fights and encounters with the law'.

LIGHTING THE WAY

The first lighthouse began operating on the Casquets in 1724. The lighthouse keeper was court-martialled for negligence in 1744 when the 100-gun warship, HMS *Victory*, disappeared in a storm, along with all 1,000 men on board. However, when divers came upon the wreck in 2008, it was 60 nautical miles from the Casquets. The construction of the Hanois Lighthouse in 1862 aided mariners negotiating the reefs. Today it throws a beam for 23 miles (37km).

The Shipwreck Museum, found within Fort Grey *(see page 48)*, tells the grim story of many of the local shipwrecks and displays their salvaged treasures. The museum could not be in a more appropriate setting: overlooking the graveyard of more than 90 recorded shipwrecks.

One of the worst disasters was the wreck of the railway steamer, SS *Stella*, which ran into fog and struck the Casquets in 1898. The boat sank within eight minutes and 105 lives were lost.

A large number of vessels were wrecked on the treacherous rocks of Les Hanois. In 1807 HMS *Boreas* sank with a loss of 127 lives. A cannon salvaged from the frigate was installed at Fort Grey and points to the Hanois reef where she foundered. A wreck with a happier ending was the SS

Above: the lighthouse on Alderney.
Right: the remains of a jar from the collection of the Shipwreck Museum.

Tour 4

Central Guernsey

A combination of retail therapy, rich heritage and coastal nature reserves makes this 13-mile (21km) tour diverse enough to suit many tastes

Traffic passing through St Peter Port is channelled along the Esplanade, then out of town along St Julian's Avenue and up to College Street, passing **St James's** church on the left. The church was built in 1818 and converted to become the island's principal concert and arts venue. It was extended to include new galleries, a café and in the basement, in a special gallery, a tapestry that took four years to make and shows scenes depicting 1,000 years of island life *(see Route 1, page 27)*.

Opposite is the neo-Gothic bulk of **Elizabeth College**, founded as a school in the 16th century and rebuilt in the 1820s using the proceeds from a special tax of a shilling on every gallon of spirits sold on the island.

Highlights

- Catherine Best Workshop
- German Underground Military Hospital
- Little Chapel
- Lihou Island
- St Apolline's Chapel

Ahead lies **Grange Road**, with fine 18th- and early 19th-century villas and terraces, many now converted to banks or guesthouses. The houses of this period on the islands have nearly all retained their ironwork around the garden and steps, unlike mainland Britain, where much architectural ironwork was removed during World War II and turned into munitions.

Above: Catherine Best's studio in a converted windmill. **Left**: walking across the Causeway to Lihou Island.

Turn left at the next junction and you will see the even grander houses that line **The Queen's Road.** The street was originally known as La Petite Marché, but was renamed when Queen Victoria visited Guernsey in 1846. All the houses are set in spacious park-like gardens, including Government House, with its sentry boxes at the gate. This was acquired by the States of Guernsey

as the residence of the island's governor after World War I.

At the next set of traffic lights, a slight detour will take you to the **Catherine Best Jewellery Workshop and Showroom ❶** (www.catherine best.com; Mon–Sat 9am–5pm, Sun 10am–4pm). Turn left, following signs to the airport, and straight on at the next junction. The second turning left, shortly after the junction, will bring you to a 19th-century mill, home to the workshop. One of the island's most creative jewellers, Catherine's pieces are often styled from rare, brilliantly coloured gemstones such as tourmaline or tanzanite. Most of the designs are limited editions.

GERMAN UNDERGROUND MILITARY HOSPITAL

Returning to the traffic lights, turn left and continue for just under a mile, until you pass a left turn with a small sign to the **German Underground Military Hospital ❷** (May–Oct daily 10am–noon and 2–4pm; Mar, Apr and Nov limited opening; charge).

Tucked away down a green rural lane, this is one of the largest complexes in the Channel Islands constructed during the Occupation era. The hospital is a testimony to Hitler's mistaken

Ⓢ Martyn Guille Silversmiths

Just beyond the main road, along a leafy path to the left, you'll find **Guernsey Clockmakers and Martyn Guille Silversmiths and Fine Jewellers** (Mon–Sat 9am–5pm, Sun 10am–4pm), where you can watch craftsmen at work and browse the showroom. Among the items made here are the famous Guernsey milk cans, Christening cups and bachins. A large range of clocks is also on display.

Above: a range of silver and gold ormer jewellery is made here.

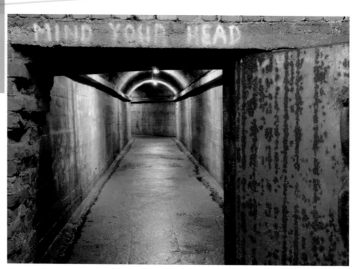

Above: the rusty door and entrance to the German Underground Military Hospital.

belief that the Allies would, as a matter of pride, eventually seek to attack and retake the Channel Islands. Hitler entrusted the task of fortifying the islands to Dr Fritz Todt, who had earlier been responsible for planning and building Germany's *autobahn* system. Organisation Todt, as it was known, involved turning the Channel Islands into an impregnable fortress, with artillery able to cover a whole sweep of the French coast.

This hospital, along with its counterpart in Jersey, was intended for the treatment of hundreds of German military casualties in the event of an attack. Built underground, the wards and operating theatres were hewn out of solid rock by slave workers from Russia, Poland, Alsace and the Czech Republic, many of whom died as a result of the brutal treatment meted out by the German Occupying Forces.

The tunnels took more than three and a half years to build but were operational for only nine months. The expected Allied invasion never came and the occupying forces surrendered

on 9 May 1945. Instead, the space was used principally to store the vast quantities of munitions stock-piled by the Germans.

Nearly all the military medical equipment was removed and as a result the Hospital is sombre and cavernous. Unlike its counterpart in Jersey there are only a handful of displays, and the dim lighting, damp concrete floors and the very emptiness of the place make it a more chilling reminder of Guernsey under the jackboot.

THE LITTLE CHAPEL

From this dank and chilly spot, go back to the main road, follow the sharp bend to the left and then take the first right turn to reach the **Little Chapel** ❸ (accessible all year). The building is a complete church in miniature, claimed to be the smallest in the world. The chapel was begun in 1923 by Brother Déodat of the De la Salle Brothers, owners of the adjoining school and estate. The building you see today is the last in a sequence of three. Déodat started work on a smaller first version in 1914 but demolished it immediately after it was built. The second one stood until 1923 and it was in the same year that he started the present chapel. In 1939 when Déodat returned to France due to ill health, the care of the chapel was entrusted to a fellow monk, Brother Cephas, who continued with the decoration until he retired in 1965. The chapel is modelled on the grotto in the Church of Lourdes and encrusted in shells, coloured pebbles and china fragments. Just 16ft (5 metres) in length, it can accommodate a dozen people.

Exiting from the car park, turn right and after about 1½ miles (2½km) you will come to another establishment where craftsmen work while you watch. Here the staff of **Bruce**

Above: the Little Chapel is now cared for by Blanchelande College.

Russell & Son Goldsmiths, Silversmiths and Jewellers ❹ (tel: 01481-264 321; www.bruce-russell. com; Mon–Sat 10am–5pm) make beautiful objects from gold, silver and platinum, including candlesticks, goblets, napkin rings and spoons, caskets and the traditional Guernsey loving cup. The family business has been going strong since 1887. Even if silversmiths are not your scene it's worth a visit for the award-winning 8-acre (3-hectare) gardens, plus coffee

Hedge Veg

As you travel around the island you are likely to see a number of 'honesty stalls', unmanned roadside booths selling home-grown fruit and veg. The stalls are an endearing feature of the island, used for disposing of surplus garden produce – from cut flowers and new potatoes to giant marrows, courgettes and asparagus. You choose what you want and leave the correct change in an honesty box.

Above: 'hedge veg' produce is often available at local honesty stalls.

and cake or a full meal at the Mint Brasserie and Tea Room *(see listing, page 61)*.

The road from here wriggles round the western end of the airport and joins the main road. Turn right to continue west, past the Longfrie Inn (where the indoor Fun Factory is a hit with youngsters) and the inconspicuous entrance to the **Coach House Gallery** (daily 10am–5pm) and a pottery workshop, both in restored farm buildings. The gallery was started in 1975 in the north of Guernsey by a group of practising artists and enthusiasts and has justifiably established a high reputation. Works on sale include watercolours and prints of Guernsey, pottery and glass.

PLEINMONT HEADLAND/ WEST COAST

At the next junction, turn left and park in the car park on the left-hand side of the road to explore the headland at the northern tip of **L'Erée Bay**.

Above: the Coach House Gallery displays and sells good-quality works.

Above: Le Creux ès Faies: a dolmen you can crawl inside.

The first site of note, just up from the car park (about 300yds/metres from L'Erée Hotel) is **Le Creux ès Faies** ❺, the island's third largest megalithic tomb. The name means 'Entrance to Fairyland' and it is not difficult to see why it got this name. The tomb is surrounded by a granite wall of alternate vertical and horizontal stones, and you can crawl into the dark interior to look up at the two massive stones capping the whole structure. The prehistoric passage grave was probably built around 3000BC and continued in use for 1,000 years or more, with bodies and ashes being placed in the chambers, along with gifts of pottery, flint and stone tools.

Uphill, just beyond the dolmen, is a pretty tea garden, where good-value sandwiches, salads, cream teas and home-baked cakes can be enjoyed. High on the headland above is **Fort Saumarez** ❻, which has the appearance of a World War II artillery control tower. The wartime structure was constructed on top of an older Martello Tower, built in 1805. The fort is named

after Lord James Saumarez, who in 1794 defeated five attacking French frigates with his ship, HMS *Crescent*.

LIHOU ISLAND

Continue downhill from the tower and you will come to another car park with a large monument commemorating those who lost their lives when MV *Prosperity* foundered on the reefs off Perelle Bay in January 1974 with the loss of all 16 crew. From the car park, a path leads down to the causeway which at low tide links mainland Guernsey to **Lihou Island** ❼. This lovely windswept islet, the most westerly point of the Channel Islands, is now a nature reserve, noted for its seabirds and wildflowers. A notice at the head of the causeway gives the times when it may safely be crossed (the tide returns swiftly, and can cut you off). You can also find the times of the tides in the *Guernsey Press* or they are available from Fort Grey. Heights of the tide may vary, and it is advisable to err on the side of caution.

For centuries the causeway was one of the main gathering places of *vraic* (pronounced 'rack') or seaweed,

Above: the German Occupation tower Fort Saumarez.

Above: the view from Guernsey across to Lihou Island, with its one and only house.

for use as a fertiliser on farmlands bordering the coast. Horses and carts were formerly used for transport, gaining access to beaches via the slipways. Today you can still see tractors loading up with the weed.

Above: little remains of Notre Dame de Lihou priory.

Apart from its wildlife, Lihou is mainly of interest for the remains of the 12th-century priory of **Notre Dame de Lihou**, built by Benedictine monks who arrived from the Abbey of Mont St Michel in around 1114. Three dolmens and seven menhirs discovered by the monks were used as foundations for the chapel. The priory is believed to have been used until the 16th century, after which it became a farmhouse. During World War II the church was used as target practice by the Germans. Little now remains of the building, except a few wall fragments. Until 1994, when the States of Guernsey bought the island from the owners for £435,000, a Guernsey law forbade all but islanders to make the crossing to Lihou. Beyond the priory, on the northwest coast, you can climb over rocks to the **Venus Pool**, large and deep enough to bathe in, but take heed of the signs discouraging access during the nesting season.

RAMSAR SITE

Lihou Island, La Claire Mare Nature Reserve and the Colin Best Nature Reserve – 1,045 acres (426 hectares) in all – were designated a Ramsar site in 2006. Ramsar is the name of an Iranian town on the southern shores of the Caspian Sea where, in 1971, 34 countries signed the Convention on Wetlands of International Importance, aimed at promoting the conservation of threatened wetlands and their resources. Guernsey's site encompasses a variety of habitats, from shingle banks to marshes, reed beds, saline lagoons and the intertidal area with its outlying reefs and rocks. The rich biodiversity of flora and fauna includes a wide range of sea birds, wild flowers and marine organisms; 214 species of seaweed have been recorded on Lihou causeway alone. The saltmarsh attracts shelduck, little ringed plover, greenshank and occasional rare migrants such as the pectoral and buff-breasted sandpiper.

The Colin Best and adjoining Claire Mare nature reserves are located east of the Fort Saumarez Headland. Yellow horned poppies grow on the landward side of the shingle bank, called **Les Anguillières**, and sea kale grows on the seaward side. The fields on the opposite side of the road served as Guernsey's first airport and alongside there is an area

Ⓕ The Guernsey Cow

Guernsey cows, with their doe eyes and dished (concave) faces, are a special breed that has been selected since the mid-19th century. Hardy, and yielding large quantities of creamy fat-rich milk, the cattle on Guernsey were widely exported in the 1920s and 1930s, and are the genetic source of herds found in Australia, New Zealand and the Americas. The purity of the breed has been guaranteed by the ban on the import of live cattle to the island. The Guernsey Dairy produces cheese, butter, ice cream and the renowned thick and golden Guernsey cream.

Above: the milk from a Guernsey cow has a high level of beta-carotene, which gives it that lovely yellow colour.

Above: the common spotted orchid flowers in July and August.

of wet meadows and ponds, a habitat for snipe, kingfishers, wagtails and warblers.

PERELLE BAY

Continuing round the headland, stop in the next car park at the southern end of **Perelle Bay**. Perelle derives from the Celtic word for rock; at low tide the bay is a rocky lunar landscape. This used to be a favourite bay for collecting ormers, the indigenous mollusc prized for its unique flavour and mother-of-pearl inner shell.

Once a staple of island dinner tables, the ormer is now a gourmet rarity, although the stocks are protected to ensure the molluscs' survival.

Cross the road to find the dolmen called **Le Trépied**. This prehistoric passage grave was reputed to be the place where local witches met with the devil for Friday-night revelries. According to confessions extracted from the "witches" at the trials in the early 17th century, the devil, in the form of a black goat, would stand on the dolmen while the witches danced round.

ST APOLLINE'S CHAPEL

At the next junction, turn right (inland) and follow the road around the sharp left-hand bend. Soon afterwards, stop to admire **St Apolline's Chapel 8** (open daylight hours). The granite chapel, built in 1394, is a single-cell building and thought to be the only remaining medieval chantry chapel in Guernsey. The fragments of frescoes are thought to depict the *Last Supper* and the *Betrayal*. The chapel had been used as a cowshed before the States of Guernsey bought it in 1873 and rescued it from this humble role. The site was restored in the 1970s as a Chapel of Unity.

Below: Le Trépied dolmen dates from the Neolithic period (4000 to 2500BC).

Above: a stained-glass window depicting St Apolline.

ST SAVIOUR

Continuing inland, take the second main turning right to follow a winding road up past **St Saviour Reservoir** ❾ to the hilltop parish church. Hikers will appreciate the pleasant 2-mile (3km) walk around the reservoir. The impressive Parish Church of St Saviour is medieval in origin, and was partly rebuilt in 1658 after the spire was struck by lightning.

Turning left will bring you to the entrance of **St Saviour's Tunnels** (closed to the public for safety reasons), a complex built during the World War II Occupation that burrows beneath St Saviour's church. The Germans chose this site for their main ammunition store, reasoning that the RAF would be unlikely to bomb a church, or even suspect what lay beneath the churchyard.

Ⓔ Eating Out

Auberge du Val
Sous L'Église, St Saviours, tel: 01481-263 862; www.aubergeduval guernsey.com; closed Sun dinner and all day Mon.
Very popular traditional *auberge* in an attractive rural setting. Ideal for a simple bistro-style lunch or more adventurous evening meals. ££

The Farmhouse
St Saviours; tel: 01481-264 181; www. thefarmhouse.gg; lunch and dinner.
In a hotel converted from an old farmhouse, the restaurant has a contemporary look and modern cuisine to match. A meal might start with a soup or seafood platter, followed by lobster and prawn linguini or free-range pork loin. Light lunches can be enjoyed by the outdoor pool in summer. ££–£££

Mint Brasserie and Tea Room
Le Gron, St Saviours (in the gardens of the Bruce Russell & Son Goldsmiths complex); tel: 01481-266 556; www.mint.gg; Jun–Sep daily

9am–5pm and dinner on Fri and Sat, off season Tues–Sun 9am–5pm.
This new farmhouse-style brasserie has won favour with its fair prices, home-made cakes and scones, and à la carte lunches and dinners. The restaurant promotes locally sourced ingredients where possible, and makes its own bread and Guernsey *gâche* (fruit loaf). Choose from fish and chips, pie of the day, pea and herb risotto or one of the substantial salads. The Sunday lunch menu offers more sophisticated fare. £–££

Taste of India
Sunset Cottage, L'Erée; tel: 01481-264 516; www.tasteofindiaci.com; lunch and dinner daily.
Stroll across the beach then stoke up at this Indian restaurant, just across from the bay, and enjoy the sunset. Expect large portions and plenty of punters. The set-price 3-course lunch with a glass of wine for under a tenner is proving very popular. Takeaways are available. £

Tour 5

Northern Guernsey

Explore the north for its fine bays, harbours and coastal forts. If you're visiting the attractions and taking breaks at beaches allow a day for this 21-mile (34km) tour

Flat northern Guernsey has an entirely different character from the southern and central uplands. Fringed by sandy beaches, the west-facing coast is backed by dunes and sandy common, too poor to farm, but now used as a public golf course. There are plenty of opportunities for bathing so bring swimming costumes and towels. Inland, the region is more heavily developed, with industrial complexes around St Sampson's and greenhouses producing cut flowers.

Highlights

- Vazon Bay
- Fort Hommet
- Cobo Bay
- Saumarez Park
- Folk and Costume Museum
- Le Déhus Dolmen

TALBOT VALLEY

Head out of St Peter Port along Grange Road and The Queen's Road, past the whitewashed stucco of Regency terraces, followed by the pink granite farmhouses as you go west past the

Princess Elizabeth Hospital. Turn right at the next major junction to drive down the green **Talbot Valley ❶**. Part of the way down this steep-sided valley, grazed by sandy-brown Guernsey cows, you will pass Guernsey's only working watermill on the left. This is one of six mills in the valley, surviving in various states of repair.

Further down on the right is a car park in an abandoned quarry and a footpath, the **Ron Short Walk**, (named after a past chairman of the Guernsey National Trust) which climbs the valley edge and affords good views over an undeveloped, peaceful and green part of Guernsey.

VAZON BAY

At the bottom of the valley, **King's Mills** is named after three watermills that once stood on this site, drawing on the power of the Talbot Valley stream. Turn left when you reach the main road, then take the next main right turn to descend to sandy **Vazon Bay** ❷, deservedly one of Guernsey's most popular beaches. Beneath the vast sands lie the remains of a submerged forest, evidence of which is exposed periodically by winter storms. The forest is thought to have been destroyed by a tidal wave

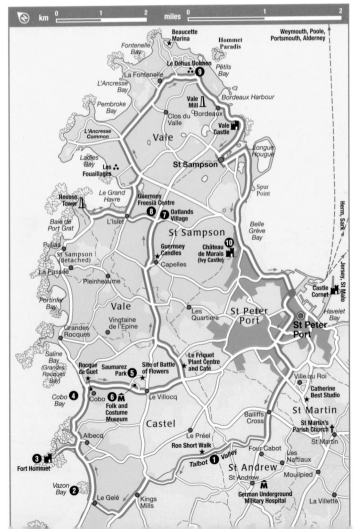

in AD709. Vazon is the sports playground of the island, where Guernsey beach boys ride the rollers and shore fishermen bring in bass and mullet. To join the fun head for the Guernsey Surf School (tel: 07911 710 789; www.guernseysurfschool.co.uk) which offers coaching for all abilities and hires out wetsuits, surf- and bodyboards, kayaks and stand-up paddleboards. As well as being a good windsurfing bay, the wide flat beach is used for motorbike racing in summer.

Fort Hommet ❸, a solidly built Martello tower of red granite, stands on the headland to the north of the bay. Wherever you find Napoleonic fortifications, there are sure to be German defences, for the Occupation troops appreciated the skills of their predecessors in finding sites from where artillery could cover a large sweep of coast. Here, a German gun casemate (Apr–Oct Tue and Sat 2–5pm; charge) has been restored.

COBO BAY

Continuing round the coast, you next come to **Cobo Bay ❹**, another fine

Above: Cobo Bay's distinctive pink granite is evident along the beach.

bathing beach, particularly popular with families. As evening falls BBQs light up along the beach, and diners gather on the terrace of the **Cobo Bay Hotel** to watch the setting sun. The distinctive pinky-red rock along the coast here is known as Cobo granite and has long been a source of

Above: Fort Hommet was stripped of all scrap metal after the war.

Ⓢ Ra-Ra Wraps

Guernsey wraps, the all-in-one beach towelling tubes, have been a tradition for islanders of all ages for over 50 years. Tying at the neck, they provide an easy and discreet way of undressing on the sands when you go for a dip at one of Guernsey's many bays. Originally all home-made, the wraps are now produced commercially – sometimes with cartoons, dragons, dolphins or other designs. The main manufacturers of the wraps are Rara at La Lisière, Bordeaux, Vale, www.rarawraps.com.

stone for buildings on the west side of the island; St Matthew's Church at the southern end of the bay is quite a striking example of its use. If you climb the steps to the top of the now-wooded quarry behind the bay, you will find the **Rocque de Guet Watchhouse and Battery**, a Napoleonic watchtower, from where there are splendid views of Vazon, Cobo and Grandes Rocques bays.

SAUMAREZ PARK

From Cobo Bay turn inland along the main road. In just over a mile (1½km), turn left at the crossroads, and left again for the main car park of **Saumarez Park ❺** (daylight hours; free; not to be confused with Sausmarez Manor in St Martin). Children are in their element here, with a big adventure playground, excellent tea-rooms and a vast park.

Saumarez Park and the imposing French-style house at its southern edge were created in the 18th century by William Le Marchant before coming, through marriage, into the hands of the de Saumarez family. The entire property was purchased in 1938 by

the States of Guernsey, and opened to the public.

The house is nowadays the Hostel of St John, used as a residential home for the elderly, with no access for the public. Formal gardens surround the house, very much in the same French idiom as the house itself. Both reflect the tastes of St James Vincent de Saumarez, the fourth lord Saumarez, who spent much of his life as a diplomat in the British Embassy in Paris. As well as formal gardens, there is a camellia lawn, bamboo walk, and Japanese walk and garden that James de Saumarez created on his return from diplomatic visits to Japan. He came back with many exotic plants – plus a Japanese carpenter and gardeners to build the Japanese temple and tend the grounds.

FOLK AND COSTUME MUSEUM

To the rear of the house, beyond the tearoom, is the National Trust of Guernsey's recently upgraded and extended **Folk and Costume**

Above: although Saumarez House is closed to the public, you can enjoy a stroll around the gardens and the park.

Above: the boat reputed to have saved 13 passengers from a shipwreck.

Museum ❻ (www.nationaltrust-gsy. org.gg; mid-Mar–Oct daily 10am– 5pm, May–Aug until 5.30pm). This excellent museum, within 18th-century farm buildings grouped around a cobbled courtyard, shows life on the island as it used to be around 100 years ago. The first part contains a series of reconstructed rooms showing a typical Guernsey farmhouse kitchen, and

Above: a mangle at the Folk and Costume Museum.

the town house parlour of a middle-class home with period costumes and furnishings. Upstairs a display on childhood includes a school room, complete with school benches.

The new costume section includes an array of 1750–1995 wedding gowns, plus fashions from 'The Party Afterwards' including a Christian Dior dress worn by the British film star Olivia De Havilland (she of *Gone with the Wind* fame, 1939). A new room showcases a splendid fully furnished scale model of a Victorian town house.

The outbuildings now display a wide range of tools and implements used in domestic and working life in Guernsey at the turn of the century. There are crab pots, fish baskets, ormering hooks, a Victorian mangle used by children doing the washing, rabbit traps and pig-killing knives, milk cans and threshing tools, old-fashioned boneshakers and carts and carriages, all giving an insight into the varied diet and the never-ending pattern of work involved in rural life. There are even some renovated pig sties.

The last display is devoted to the once-flourishing tomato industry.

a huge and colourful garden centre, with a children's play area and a regular programme of free events.

This is just one of a cluster of attractions in the vicinity that are ideal for rainy days. Turning right from Le Friquet, and right at the next junction, you will pass three further attractions. **Guernsey Candles** (tel: 01481-249 686; daily 9am–5pm) has candles in every conceivable shape and size as well as displays on the intricacies of the candlemaking craft.

At the next junction, the right turn will take you to **Oatlands Village** ❼ (www.oatlands.gg, daily 9.30am–

Above: fisherman's smock at the Folk and Costume Museum.

Guernsey's first glasshouses, built in 1792, were used for growing dessert grapes but became a source of huge wealth as tomatoes, introduced in 1865, took over. Until the 1960s the sweet, juicy and flavoursome Guernsey toms (along with Jersey Royal potatoes) were eagerly awaited by many people as early-season crops. In 1957 more than 9 million 12lb (5kg) trays of tomatoes were exported. But what was once a staple of English grocers was driven out of the market by Dutch imports, and today Guernsey toms are virtually unavailable off the island.

The boat in the courtyard outside was reputed to have saved 13 passengers from the SS *Stella* which hit the rocks off Alderney in March 1899, with the loss of 105 passengers and crew.

RETAIL THERAPY

Turn left out of the museum and at the second crossroads left turn for **Le Friquet Plant Centre and Café** (www.lefriquetgardencentre. gg; Mon–Thur 8.30am–6pm, Fri–Sat 8.30am–8pm, Sun 10am–5pm),

ⓕ Becoming a Local

If you fall in love with Guernsey, and fancy living here, you need to be rich. A glance at estate agents' windows will reveal that there are two types of property on the market: reasonably priced accommodation and the phenomenally expensive. One two-bedroom apartment may be priced at £350,000, whilst its identical neighbour costs £1 million. The reason is that the cheaper apartment can only be bought by a Guernsey native, whilst the millionaires' property is for sale on the open market. By this means, Guernsey controls migration to the islands, which would otherwise be flooded by tax exiles.

Above: a charming cottage with tile roof will require deep pockets.

Facts and Fun at the Folk Museum

To keep children occupied at the Folk and Costume Museum there are two sets of work sheets, one for the under 10s, and another for 10–13 year olds. Youngsters fill in the forms as they go round the museum, spotting the relevant items and collecting facts and figures. Those who correctly fill in the sheets receive small prizes. Work sheets are usually handed out at the entrance; if not, ask on arrival.

Above: handmade dolls on display at the Folk and Costume Museum.

5pm) with attractions for all ages. Gift shops and craft workshops are grouped around a courtyard set in converted brickworks, complete with bottle-shaped kilns. Diverse attractions over the 5-acre (2-hectare) site include an attractively landscaped mini-golf course, a Jungle House play area (charge) with a soft play zone and eight full-size trampolines, Junior Go-Karts, Guernsey

Goldsmiths, a large craft and hobbies shop, a *chocolatier* and a variety of eateries.

At the same crossroads, the left turn takes you to the **Guernsey Freesia Centre** ❽ (daily 10am–5pm), where you can see freesias at different stages of bloom. You can also arrange to have flowers sent to friends and family at home. Guernsey produces two thirds of all freesias sold to mainland Britain, along with huge numbers of roses. Apparently the high light levels enjoyed by the island encourage the growth of long straight stems – perfect for cut flowers. Depending on the time of your visit you can see the various growing stages of the freesia, the planting of corms and the picking, bunching and boxing of the flowers.

GRAND HAVRE AND L'ANCRESSE

Due north of the Freesia Centre is the sheltered and sandy beach at **Le Grand Havre**, separated by an area of seaweed-covered rocks from the equally attractive **Ladies' Bay**. White sands here are only fully revealed in their glory when tides are low. While here, you can visit the **Rousse Tower**, which stands on the

Above: the Oatlands kiln is a reminder of the once-thriving brick industry.

Above: the Guernsey Freesia Centre is mainland Britain's key supplier.

headland to the west of Le Grand Havre. One of a chain of 15 towers built in the 1780s against the threat of invasion by France, it has been fully restored and contains displays on the history of Napoleonic-era fortifications on Guernsey.

From the high points on **L'Ancresse Common,** at the very northern end of the island, you can see many such fortifications. Here the horizon bristles with tall circular towers and square forts, spaced at regular intervals, each one guarding a possible landing site and intended as a show of strength to deter Napoleon from planning an invasion. Far harder to see is the oldest prehistoric site on Guernsey, hidden among the gorse and bracken on the southern edge of the common (ask a golfer for directions to the fifth hole). Named **Les Fouaillages**, this roofless burial chamber, consisting of a ring of fallen stones, was constructed more than 6,000 years ago and only rediscovered in 1976.

Sandy **Pembroke** and **L'Ancresse bays** provide the last opportunities for bathing, as the island's northern road fringes the common and turns south. From here on, the beaches are subject to fast currents – more appealing for rock pooling and birdwatching.

LE DÉHUS DOLMEN

Just after the road turns south, look for a narrow lane on the left which leads to **Le Déhus Dolmen ❾** (open all hours), Guernsey's most

Above: the Rousse tower and battery are a uniquely combined structure.

ⓥ Vale Castle

Between Bordeaux and St Sampson's harbours, just inland from the main road, lie the hilltop relics of **Vale Castle**. The earliest occupant of the hill is believed to have been a double-banked hill-fort dating from the Iron Age. The first medieval fort was erected in around 1400. Barracks were constructed during the Napoleonic Wars but demolished by the Germans during the Occupation. It's worth walking up to the top for the fine views of all the Channel Islands.

Above: Vale Castle has been used as a military site for more than 2,000 years.

atmospheric passage grave. Not only is the dolmen perfectly preserved, with a small wooden door for an entrance, it is also furnished with an electric light. Turning on this light throws into relief a mysterious carving on the underside of one of the tomb's massive capstones: the figure of a bearded man, armed with bow and arrows, known as the Guardian of Le Déhus. Some scholars have suggested that the figure was already carved on the stone before it was incorporated into the tomb. If so, it would predate the construction of the dolmen, which is itself more than 4,000 years old.

Continuing south, you will see the tall tower of **Vale Mill** (1850) high on a hillock over to the right as you skirt the fishing port at Bordeaux Harbour. Originally a flour windmill, the occupying Germans used it as an anti-aircraft position.

ST SAMPSON

The former industrial hub of the island has been spruced up in recent years. Although still a commercial working harbour with shipyards, power station, oil tankers and coal docks, it has a modern well-equipped marina, and attracts visitors for its many duty-free outlets and restaurants, ranged along the harbour front. It is best known for its jewellers, particularly **Ray & Scott**, who specialise in diamonds and have their own diamond museum (Mon–Sat 9.30am–5pm).

Left: the passage grave at Le Déhus Dolmen is lit for visitors.

The town is named after **St Sampson** who was born in Wales and moved to Brittany where he founded a monastery and became Bishop of Dol in around AD550. He travelled from Brittany to Guernsey and is believed to have landed in the natural harbour that now bears his name. He brought Christianity to Guernsey and is said to have founded a chapel where the parish church of St Sampson's now stands. Today's church was built in 1111, and originally stood on the seashore.

As a last stop, before returning to St Peter Port, look out for the Château de Marais standing on the edge of a drab housing estate inland from Belle Grève Bay. Known locally as the **Ivy Castle** ❿ (open daylight hours) it is no longer ruined and ivy-clad, but has been well restored to illustrate a sequence of defences, from the 13th-century moated bailey to the 18th-century powder magazine and the inevitable concrete bunker, built when the Germans re-fortified the castle during World War II.

Ⓔ Eating Out

The Beach House
Pembroke Bay, Vale; tel: 01481-246 494; www.beachhouseguernsey.com; open all day in season.
A café and restaurant right on the beach in a stark modern building, with a viewing gallery for meals above. Open for breakfast through to dinner. £–££

Cobo Bay Restaurant
Cobo Bay Hotel, Cobo Bay; tel: 01481-257 102; www.cobobayhotel. com; lunch and dinner except Jan and Feb when closed for lunch.
The panoramic windows of this seaside hotel make the most of the beach views and sunsets. Start with diver-caught scallops wrapped in pancetta and follow with chargrilled beef fillet or home-made veal burger. The restaurant has won awards for the quality of food and service. ££–£££

Cobo Fish and Chip Bar
Cobo Bay; tel: 01481-254 276.
Buy fish and chips from this basic but popular chippie and enjoy them while watching the glorious sunset over Cobo Bay across the road. £

Crabby Jacks
Vazon Bay, Castel; tel: 01481-257 489; www.crabbyjacksrestaurant.com; open daily noon–late, also 9am–noon at weekends for brunch.

A casual seaside bar and bistro popular with surfers and families for its large helpings of steaks and burgers, and at night for its fabulous sunset view and dancing at weekends. £

Fleur du Jardin
Kings Mill, Castel, tel: 01481-257 996; www.fleurdujardin.com; lunch and dinner.
This country hotel produces first-class, simply cooked gastro pub fare, with an emphasis on local produce. Expect Guernsey-bred beef and pork, freshly caught seabass, west coast scallops or a locally sourced crab sandwich. Regarded by many as the best dining pub in the Channel Islands. £–££

Port Soif Kiosk and Tea Garden
Port Soif, Vale.
Excellent value home-made food including bacon butties, fresh crab sandwiches and generously buttered Guernsey *gâche*. £

Vistas Beach Cafe
Vazon Bay; tel: 01481-252 513.
After several years of running their business from portacabins during a battle with the planning authorities, Vistas (formerly the Vazon Beach Café) has finally reopened in modern new premises. Simple wholesome food and great views of surfers and sunsets. £–££

Tour 6

Herm

This diminutive island with enticing beaches and no cars makes a wonderful day or half-day trip from Guernsey. The 3-mile (5km) walk covers most of the island

Herm is a tiny holiday island measuring just 1½ miles (2½km) long and ½-mile (1km) wide. Visitors come for the scenery, the swimming, the walking and the wildlife. It's also a favourite of foodies who come over from Guernsey for lunch or on the early evening boat to enjoy freshly caught lobster or Sark lamb.

Freedom from consumer values is what makes Herm so appealing and, with a ban on cars, radios played in public and unseemly behaviour, this really is the place to get away. The best way to enjoy all this peace is to walk around the island.

Beach lovers begin to arrive in mid-morning in summer, heading for the broad swathes of sandy beach to the north and east. Although the island

Highlights

- Fisherman's Beach
- Shell Beach
- Belvoir Bay
- St Tugual's chapel

has enough paths and beaches to absorb most of the tourists, try and avoid Sundays when up to 2,000 day-trippers arrive from Guernsey.

The only way of getting to Herm is by boat. Travel Trident passenger ferries (tel: 01481-721 379, www.traveltrident.com) depart from St Peter Port harbour and take 20 minutes. Tickets can be bought at the Trident kiosk by Weighbridge Clock Tower (near the Liberation

Monument) or from the boat crew as you board. In July and August ferries depart eight times daily from 8.30am–5.15pm. Boats run all year but there is a reduced service off-season, and services are dependent on the weather. Last boats back are at around 5pm but there are special seasonal 'dinner boats' returning at 10.45pm if you want to go for an evening meal. For all other information on Herm, visit www.herm.com.

HERM HARBOUR

At high tide ferries dock in Herm's small harbour, while at low tide passengers disembark at the Rosaire Steps before making their way along the track to the harbour – which is the hub of the island. The long-established **White House Hotel** ❶, overlooking gardens and beach, is a country house hotel with an old-fashioned charm and sense of decorum. Guests dress for dinner and are invited for drinks at the Monk's Bar overlooking the gardens before dining. A stay here is an escape from the 21st century – there are no televisions or telephones in the bedrooms and no clocks on the walls.

From the harbour, a broad level path leads left, passing the **Mermaid Tavern** ❷. This was originally a fishermen's pub, now it is the social centre of the island. The path was once a railway that carried stone from the island's numerous quarries to cargo boats in the harbour. Herm's granite was said to be the hardest and best of all stone quarried in the Channel Islands in the 19th century. It was used for railway construction as well as for more prestigious projects: in London, the Duke of York steps, leading off Pall Mall, and the steps up to St Paul's Cathedral are both made of Herm granite.

To the left, as you follow the path, is **Fisherman's Beach** ❸, a fine

Left: the Rosaire Steps.
Above: Fisherman's Beach.

stretch of sand at low tide, when you can also see the weed-covered crates in which Herm's oysters are grown. The first main landmark on the north-wards route is a small cemetery containing two graves and an almost indecipherable inscription; local legend has it that this is the grave of a mother and child who died of cholera in the early 19th century, buried here by the crew of a passing ship.

HERM COMMON

Much older tombs lie scattered around **Herm Common** ❹, at the north end of the island, but it is not easy to distinguish them from natural scatters of rock, since these Neolithic tombs, dating from the period 3,500 to 2,000BC, have all collapsed – only the regularity of the stones, lying in a rough circle, indicates the site of a former tomb chamber.

There were once so many tombs here that archaeologists think Herm was used as a burial isle for members of Breton nobility. Most were lost over time to 19th-century quarrymen; the big granite capstones of the Neolithic passage graves were easy picking.

The common has more than 450 species of wild flowers. It is covered in burnet rose, a rare plant that enjoys the Herm environment, as well as all kinds of other wild flowers, from massed primroses in spring, to fuschia-pink foxglove spires in summer, and more exotic plants like New Zealand flax and Japanese cactus.

The needle-shaped monument at the northernmost point of the island marks the position of one of the

Above: the Pierre aux Rats obelisk sits on the northern shore of Herm.

island's more famous dolmens, called the **Pierre aux Rats**. When quarrymen destroyed the massive grave, the local seamen were incensed at the loss of such an important landmark

---

ⓢ Gearing up for the Beach

If you come to Herm unprepared for the beach, head for the shop near the harbour where you can buy swimming costumes, snorkels, skimboards, fishing gear and other beach paraphernalia, all at reasonable cost. Don't forget suntan lotion – Herm has the highest incidence of sunburn in the Channel Islands. The post office here sells Herm stamps, which have become collectors' items. The Guernsey PO took over Herm's postal services in 1969 and Guernsey stamps are nowadays used for post from the island.

Above: local stores can provide everything you need for a day on the beach.

and navigational aid, so the obelisk was erected in its place.

SHELL BEACH AND BELVOIR BAY

Over to the right lies **Shell Beach** ❺, backed by dunes where prickly sea hollies grow. With almost ¾ mile (1km) of golden sands and superb swimming, this is considered by some to be the Channel Islands' best beach. It consists almost entirely of shells, though most have been pulverised to fragments of sand by centuries of wave action. Each tide brings in a new crop of delicate pink, yellow and luminescent shells to keep beachcombers happy. As you explore, however, you will discover that Shell Beach is by no means unique: all the island's beaches have a large amount of shells, as does the island soil – Herm is just one big trap for exotic shells washed here from warmer waters by strong currents and the action of the Gulf Stream.

The clear and shallow waters retreat far out at low tide, making swimming safe for children. Beach cafés both here and at Belvoir Bay sell snacks, deliciously creamy ice

Above: the calm waters and white sands of Shell Beach.

creams and all the essential beach paraphernalia.

If you continue round the coast, you will come to **Belvoir Bay** ❻. This has a smaller but more sheltered beach than those further north, and has lovely views of Sark and (on a clear day) France. It is perfect for swimming but the sands can get very crowded in summer. From here you can head

Above: a footpath leads through wild flowers down to Belvoir Bay.

Above: on foot is the only way to get around the island.

south along the undulating (and at times steep) cliff path, which encircles the island and gives access to some of the best birdwatching points.

WILDLIFE

Even if you are not a bird lover before you go to Herm you may well become one once you reach the island – it is a good idea to take binoculars and a bird identification book. The island is especially rich in birdlife during the spring and autumn migration periods, when the Channel Islands serve as a feeding ground for birds of passage. During spring and summer, the whole island is alive with the vibrant song of larks, wrens and warblers. The cliffs to the south of the island attract nesting puffins and fulmars, while the sand dunes to the north are home to a colony of sand martins and, if you arrive by the early morning boat before the beaches become crowded, you will see whole flocks of oyster catchers, probing the sands for food with their bright orange beaks. In spring and early summer the local branch of the RSPB (www.rspb

guernsey.co.uk) organises puffin patrols and trips to Herm or you can take a two-hour puffin-watching kayak tour (www.outdoorguernsey.co.uk) starting at Shell Beach. The distinctive, large-beaked residents have been spotted on every patrol since 2007.

Also keep an eye out for the grey seals and bottlenose and common dolphins that have made their home in the northern rocky outcrop called The Humps.

Above: puffins breed on Jethou and Herm from April to mid-July.

MANOR VILLAGE

An alternative to going south along the cliff path is to head up the steep track to the huddle of granite houses at the centre of the island on the brow of the hill. The tower at the summit serves as a landmark as you climb. The tower and manor are the work of Prince Blücher von Wahlstatt, a wealthy and eccentric German aristocrat, the son of the Prussian Field Marshal Gebhard Blücher who fought with Wellington at Waterloo. He fell in love with the place in 1890 and bought the island lease. The prince introduced many trees to the island along with a colony of wallabies, which bred successfully but have since vanished. Sadly, the prince was interned at the outbreak of World War I and never returned to Herm.

A subsequent tenant was the novelist, Sir Compton Mackenzie, best remembered for *Whisky Galore* (1928) who lived here from 1920 until he retired to the neighbouring island of Jethou. He was succeeded by Lord Perry, the chairman of Ford who once lived in The White House Hotel and gave it its unique name 'in homage to his transatlantic connections'. Lampposts and cottage fronts were once painted bright blue or orange – the colours of the Ford Motor Company.

F Idyllic Island

Herm has a resident population of just 66. There are no nurses or doctors, although there are set procedures and selected people to deal with emergencies. Motorised vehicles are banned, with the exception of three tractors, one Land Rover and a handful of quad bikes for the locals. You can't own a house on Herm, play a radio in public areas or pick the flowers. Troublemakers used to be interned in the tiny beehive-shaped prison in the grounds of the White House Hotel. Today they are shipped back to Guernsey and the prison is used to store lawnmowers.

Above: unlike the other Channel Islands, bicycles are banned on Herm.

Post-War Herm

During the war, the island escaped fortification, and was largely left to decay, so that the first post-war tenant spent a small fortune restoring the island farms. Even so, much remained to be done when Peter and Jenny Wood became tenants in 1949. The story of how they fell in love with Herm and worked to create the thriving island economy of today, based on the twin pillars of tourism and farming, is told in the late Jenny Wood's delightful book, *Herm, Our Island Home*, available from the gift shop at Herm Harbour.

ST TUGUAL

A cluster of farm buildings and cottages lies at the top of the hill, among them the tiny junior school. A teacher commutes from Guernsey daily, in all weathers, to teach the handful of pupils. Nearby you can visit the enchanting little Norman chapel of **St Tugual** ❼ whose pretty garden has a memorial to Peter and Jenny Wood, former tenants of the island *(see box, above)*. The chapel is a reminder of the days when Herm was a religious outpost, run by Catholic monks who founded a monastery and improved the land so

it could fatten livestock and produce grain. The chapel was designed so that the monks could sit in the nave, out of sight of the congregation. When Prince Blücher von Wahlstatt *(see previous page)* arrived on the island, he found the structure in a state of disrepair. He restored the building and reopened it as a chapel.

St Tugual remains an enigma. Rumour has it that the saint was a Welsh woman who accompanied St Magloire to Guernsey and Herm in the 6th century, who died here and whose memory was perpetuated by the building of the shrine. The Wood family restored the chapel and it is used for a service at 10am most Sundays. If you would like to play the organ, speak to the manager of the White House Hotel.

LE MANOIR

Turn right out of the chapel, retracing your steps past the dismembered tractors. Turn right, up the hill. At the gate to **Le Manoir** ❽ (The Manor House) is a reminder that oxen were once used as draft animals before Lord Perry introduced the first tractors. The **oxen stocks** were used to hold the animals while they were shod, since, unlike horses, bullocks are unable to stand on three legs, and need supporting.

Below: St Tugual church dates from the 10th century.

Above: climbing the Rosaire Steps after disembarking from the ferry.

have been built by the medieval monks who farmed the land on Herm until the 16th-century Dissolution. The monks also built the walls of massive granite boulders that line the spine road crossing the centre of the island.

Follow the road and you will pass the island's campsite on your left and eventually rejoin the coastal path at the southern tip of the island. Turn right here, enjoying the views across to Jethou, and you will come to **Rosaire Steps** ❾ used by Herm ferries as an alternative landing point when the receding tide makes it impossible to use the main harbour. The path now skirts the gardens of the White House Hotel, backed by the cliffs formed by quarrying activity in the 19th century. Drunken quarrymen were incarcerated in the small **gaol** by the tennis courts on the grounds of the hotel, which merits inclusion in the *Guinness Book of Records* as Britain's smallest gaol.

Alongside the manor you will see another tower, made romantic with fairy-tale turrets, that was once the island's mill. Like the chapel, it may

E Eating Out

Conservatory Restaurant
White House Hotel, Herm Harbour; tel: 01481-750 075; usually daily for lunch and dinner.
Traditional hotel restaurant where you can enjoy a whole fresh lobster, surf and turf or a Sunday lunch of British beef and Yorkshire pud and sticky toffee pudding, and listen to live harp music. Meals on the lawn in fine weather. Extensive wine list, with many brought directly from Bordeaux châteaux. ££–£££

Mermaid Tavern
Herm Harbour, tel: 01481-710 170; Apr–Oct daily, restricted times off-season.
The social hub of the island, with pub lunches and a good choice of beers and wines. This is the venue of the occasional real ale and cider festivals. At the Black Rock Grill (evenings

only, reservations on 01481-750 050) steak and fish are cooked on volcanic rocks at your table. The meat choice ranges from beef fillet to camel and kangeroo. £–££

The Ship Inn Brasserie
White House Hotel, Herm Harbour, tel: 01481-750 075; open in season daily from 9am.
Serving excellent cuisine from the kitchens of The White House Hotel, the Ship Inn has an informal atmosphere, with no dress or age restrictions. Come for a fry-up breakfast, seafood or sandwich lunches, cake and cream teas or full dinners with good-value wines. Meals can be taken alfresco on the patio, in the bar by the log fire or in the restaurant. Reservations can be made for the Trident ferry to take you back to Guernsey at 10.45pm. £–££

Fishing

For Channel Islanders fishing has always been a way of life. Lobster, crab and scallops, along with bass, brill and bream, are still all caught offshore and end up gracing the table

The limpet shells discovered at La Houge Bie, a Neolithic passage grave in Jersey, are evidence that even back in prehistoric times the islanders were enjoying their seafood.

During the Middle Ages eel was a favourite dish; the drying, salting and export of conger eels was the main industry of the Channel Islands and led to Jersey's nickname of 'Isle of the Congers'. In the 16th century canny islanders recognised the riches of the cod banks of Newfoundland, and made fortunes by sailing to Spain with huge quantities of dried cod, returning to the islands with fruit and wine. The home fisheries consequently declined but the industry was revived in the late 18th century when oysters were discovered and exported in huge quantities to England.

THE SHELLFISH FLEETS

Fishermen gradually turned their focus to lobster and crabs. String upon string of baited lobster pots were lowered to the kelp-covered reefs by fishermen from sturdy crabbers; then bigger

SEA ANGLING

Sea angling is now a major leisure activity. The Bailiwick of Guernsey has about one fifth of all British shore records; Alderney has an international reputation as a shore fishing centre where record-breaking ballan wrasse and monster grey mullet are landed. April to September are the best months for serious boat fishing. Depending on the tides you could be bank fishing for turbot, bass and brill, wrecking for cod, conger and ling or reef fishing for pollack, bream or bass. Late summer or early autumn are ideal for shore fishing for bream, bass, sole, red mullet, triggerfish, plaice, wrasse, conger and garfish, while autumn to early winter is best for wrasse and mullet.

LOW-WATER FISHING

Rock pools are a haven for crabs, crayfish, shrimp and devil fish. At strictly enforced times of the year you can seek out the ormer, valued by locals for their meat and by tourists for their fine mother-of-pearl interior shells. At very low tide you can sprinkle salt on the key-holed burrows of razor fish, wait for them to pop up (they will think the tide is in), then pull them from their holes.

boats ventured further afield, seeking their valuable quarry in the English Channel and even off the Scottish coast.

The 1960s saw the shellfish boom, with lobsters and crabs fetching high prices in top-end restaurants. Crabbers still bring in the shellfish, but meanwhile other forms of commercial fishing, such as trawling, have declined. This has, however, been good news for the sea angler.

Above: creels are used to bring in the catch on a number of local fishing boats.
Left: freshly caught mackerel ready for the markets and stalls of Guernsey.

Tour 7

Sark

Step back in time and spend a day on this idyllic island. Motorised traffic (apart from tractors) is banned, so hire a bike for this 10-mile (16km) tour, or trust to your own feet

Victor Hugo considered Sark to be *'la plus belle'* of the Channel Islands. See if you agree by taking a day trip to the island, or go for an overnight stay. Ferries to the island are run by the Isle of Sark Shipping Company and depart from St Peter Port on Guernsey, taking 50 minutes. Spring and early autumn are good times to visit, although Sark is very popular with families in the summer months. Queue early if you want outside seating on the ferry. In high season there are several boats a day, but it's wise to book ahead, especially if you decide to day trip on the cheaper 'early bird' sailing, departing at 8am and returning at 4pm or 6pm (tel: 01481-724 059 or online at www.sarkshippingcompany. com). If you decide to stay on the

Highlights

• St Peter's Church
• La Seigneurie Gardens
• La Coupée
• Silver mines
• Venus Pool

island there are plenty of options, from comfortable hotels to B&Bs to self-catering cottages. If you're looking for a more basic option, there are a couple of attractive campsites.

Sark is a small peaceful island with the atmosphere of Victorian England, and that's what attracts visitors. It has a population of 600 and the head of its government (or Chief Pleas) is the seigneur, who rides a bike. Sark's constitution dates back to 1563, when Helier de Carteret was granted sovereignty over the island in return for maintaining a militia, whose chief task was to keep the island free of the pirates who had been using Sark as a base from which to harass English shipping. Helier took 40 Jerseymen with him to colonise the uninhabited island. He divided Sark into 40 parcels of land and granted perpetual tenancy to the occupants in return for their help in defending the island. These tenements, as they are known, have remained virtually unchanged. The feudal form of government set up in Elizabeth I's reign prevailed right up until 2008 when the island held its first general election and Sark became Europe's newest democracy.

Above: the Isle of Sark. **Left**: long-lining a horse through Sark's lanes.

BRECQHOU ISLAND

The ferry passes south of Herm before swinging northwards past the rocky islet of **Brecqhou ❶**. This was sold by Dame Sybil Hathaway, the most famous ruler of Sark, in 1929 for £3,000 and purchased in 1993 for a reputed £2 million as a private tax haven by the reclusive billionaire Barclay brothers, best known as owners of the Telegraph media group and The Ritz. To the shock and horror of the Sarkese, the tycoon twins created a massive mock-Gothic castle on the island,

Above: Sark Shipping Company ferry arriving at Maseline Harbour.

ⓖ On Your Bike

Sark is only 3 miles long and 1½ miles wide (5km by 2.5km), so on a bike you can explore it all in a day. Bikes can be hired cheaply from Avenue Cycle Hire on The Avenue. In season it's best to book in advance (Avenue Cycle Hire, tel: 01481-832 102; www.avenuecycles sark.co.uk or A to B Cycles, tel: 01481-832 844; www.atobcycles. com). Apart from the occasional steep hill, pedalling is easy going. To explore some of the bays and rocky shores you have to leave the bike (no need to lock up) and continue on foot. If you're scrambling around the coastline do be aware of the state of the tide.

Above: cyclists taking in the view from Sark across to Brecqhou.

complete with 100ft (30-metre) -high granite walls, battlements and helipad. The castle is clearly visible as the ferry swings to the north of Sark. There is no public access except for those who stay at least two nights at one of the Barclay brothers' hotels on Sark, which entitles them to a complimentary trip to the Brecqhou gardens.

Having bought the property, the brothers were forced to pay the seigneur of Sark his *Treizième* or one-thirteenth of the purchase price of a tenement, under Sark's jurisdiction over Brecqhou. The brothers were also dismayed to learn that, under Sark law, they were obliged to leave the estate to an eldest son. Demanding the right to bequeath the property to all four of their children, they threatened to take the battle to the European Court of Human Rights. In 1999 the Chief Pleas caved in and updated the constitution.

In 2008, against the wishes of the majority of the islanders, the Barclay brothers instigated the first full election on Sark. Up until then the Chief Pleas (Sark's government) had mainly comprised members who had inher-

Above: climbing a coastal pathway gives an excellent view across to Brecqhou.

ited their seats under the island's 450-year-old feudal system of government. When the majority of voters rejected the Barclay brothers' preferred candidates and their manager in Sark lost his seat in the new Chief Pleas office, they withdrew their £5-million annual investment in Sark. Their family businesses on the island, including two hotels, a pub and shops, were temporarily shut down and Sark workers laid off.

The bitter feud continues, particularly between the Sarkese and the Barclays' chief lieutenant on the island who produces the controversial Sark Newsletter with personal accusations against the island's local politicians. The Barclays own around a quarter of Sark and continue to seek the full defeudalisation of the island. In 2012 de UK Minister of State for Justice, Lord McNally, informed the brothers that the UK would not let them turn the tiny island into a 'company town'.

ARRIVAL IN SARK

The ferry comes in close beneath Sark's towering cliffs, past rocks where cormorants and shags launch themselves on fishing flights. As you approach the harbour, you may see fishermen laying crab and lobster pots, and numerous sea caves and evocatively shaped rocks.

From the sea there are fews signs of human habitation, for Sark's houses lie mainly at the centre of the island, in a sheltered hollow, hidden from sight as you approach by sea. Settlers here in the 16th century built their homes as far inland as they could to shelter from the elements and from unwelcome visitors. To this day, most of the Sarkese live without a sea view.

If you're staying on the island, luggage will be carried off the boat by

Above: the 'toast rack' will carry you from the harbour up the steep hill.

Above: horse and carriage, the only other approved form of transport.

a team of porters who will take it to your accommodation. Make sure your bags are labelled clearly with your name and accommodation.

To reach the main village, you can either hop on the 'toast rack' – an open-sided tractor-drawn cart, which makes light of the short but steep haul up Harbour Hill – or take the pretty woodland footpath which runs alongside the road. At the top of the hill, footpath and road merge at the Bel Air pub. Alongside is the granite engine shed that houses Sark's electricity generator.

HORSE-DRAWN CARRIAGES

At La Collinette, just beyond the toast-rack stop, the island's famous horse-drawn carriages patiently wait to take visitors on tours around Sark (£15 per person for a minimum hour and a half in a six-seater). If you decide on this form of transport you will be looked after for the next 1–2 hours as the knowledgeable (but not necessarily Sarkese) guide takes you to the island's main sights. (In high season you can pre-book an island tour when booking the ferry crossing.) Formerly

the only powered vehicles permitted on the island were the invalid car belonging to Dame Sybil Hathaway and the tractor attached to an ambulance-van for medical emergencies. There are now more than 70 tractors, which are used for agricultural purposes and cargo deliveries. The doctor visits his patients by tractor and the ambulance is still the back end of a conventional ambulance towed by a tractor. For visitors, horse-drawn carriages are the only kind of transport allowed, apart from bikes. For the more energetic, cycling is the best way to see Sark, especially as not all the horse-drawn carriages can cross the narrow isthmus of La Coupée to Little Sark. Since this is not a round-the-island tour (there is no main coastal footpath) the suggested tour of 10 miles (16km) can easily be cut for those who prefer a shorter route.

BIG SARK

Sark's main road, **The Avenue ➋**, is lined by souvenir shops and café/bistros that are open all day for snacks and casual meals. If you are planning a picnic, you can find provisions at one

Above: St Peter's is the last church in England to rent pews, although the price has not increased since 1820.

of the food stores here. (Note that although there are two banks, Sark has no ATMs. Most of the shops and restaurants, however, take credit and debit cards, and some operate a cash-back system for up to £50.)

The Avenue divides the island into two halves — to the north are the La Seigneurie Gardens, to the south, wooded lanes lead to La Coupée, the vertiginous land bridge linking what are often described as the separate islands of Little and Big Sark.

At the top of the Avenue, by the Post Office, turn right and continue right at the next junction. You will shortly come to **St Peter's Church** ❸, built in 1820. The simple building has stained-glass windows of various saints, including St Magloire, who came from Dol in Brittany in 565 to found a monastery on Sark. The monastery flourished, supporting 62 monks and serving as a school for the children of the Breton nobility, until marauding Viking pirates destroyed the buildings and killed the monks in the 9th century.

Turn right out of the church, and after the Old Island Hall on the same side of the road you'll pass a stone building which houses the **Assembly Room** where the Chief Pleas'

ⓖ Island Wildlife

Sark's isolated position brings a wealth of wildlife. Among the species you are likely to see along the rugged coast are puffins, shags, guillemots, razorbills and oyster catchers. For the best sightings bring your binoculars and take a trip around the island with local fisherman, George Guille. You will sail past spectacular rock formations, visit caves with deep, clear water and secret beaches and coves that can only be reached by sea. Boat trips are best taken on a calm day when the caves are accessible. Trips depart from Creux Harbour at 11am and must be pre-booked at the Sark Visitor Centre (email: office@sark.co.uk or telephone 01481-832 345).

Above: a local advertisement for a group bird-watching tour around the island.

meetings take place four times a year. Sark's feudal state came to an end in 2008 when the Chief Pleas was reformed and Sark held its first election (see page 83). Continuing along the road you will see on the left the new **Island Hall** ❹ which, with its indoor sports (badminton, pool, indoor bowling, snooker and table tennis), cafè and bar, serves as a centre for much of Sark's social life.

LA SEIGNEURIE GARDENS

A little further north, you will be sharing the road with horses and carriages heading to and from **La Seigneurie Gardens** ❺ (www.laseigneurie gardens.com; Easter–Oct daily 10am–5pm; charge, guided tours every Wed at 11.30am), home of the Seigneur of Sark, Michael Beaumont (grandson of Dame Sybil Hathaway) who kindly allows public access to the garden of his 17th-century home. Although Sark is no longer a feudal state and the powers of the seigneur are much eroded, he still holds the island in perpetuity for the Crown, sits in the court of

Above: gates decorate the entrance to the gardens at La Seigneurie.

Chief Pleas and pays the Queen an annual rent of £1.79.

The sheltered **walled gardens** are packed with colourful flowers and shrubs, including climbing roses and exotic plants such as gazanias, canna lilies and bottle-brush plants from New Zealand that flourish in the frost-free island environment. The house itself (not open to the public) is no less exotic, with the Dutch gables of its Victorian wing added to the origi-

Above: the high walls around La Seigneurie Gardens protect delicate flowers.

Above: Point Robert Lighthouse stands guard on the cliffs of Sark.

nal house of 1732 and a large watch-tower built, so it is said, for sending signals to Guernsey in 1854.

To the rear of the great house is the Battery, where a cider apple crusher and several historic cannons are displayed alongside an ornate tower, and a turreted 18th-century dovecote. Until relatively recently one of the seigneur's sole privileges was to keep pigeons and doves, which fed freely and with impunity on the crops of the tenants. There is also a small area of woodland to explore, with a series of duck-filled ponds, a maze and a plant stall.

PORT DU MOULIN AND THE LIGHTHOUSE

A short way along the track north of La Seigneurie is a left turn that leads down, through woods, to **Port du Moulin** (once the site of a water-mill), with its fine coastal scenery. Just before you get to the beach, look out for the artificial 'Window in the Rock', a square hole perhaps cut through the cliff to allow carts to descend to the beach and gather *vraic*, or seaweed, used for fertilising the seigneur's fields and garden. Returning to the main track, you can turn left and continue to the end of the road to **L'Eperquerie Common**, at the northern tip of the

island, named after the poles *(perques)* once erected here for drying fish.

Coming back, turn left down Rue de Fort, to the Napoleonic-era defensive works at **La Tour**, then head south, back towards the centre of the island. Take the second left turn, which leads past the Mermaid Tavern down to Point Robert and Sark's **lighthouse** ❻ (closed to the public). It was built in 1912 and stands halfway down the cliff into which it nestles, via a flight of 165 steps, but still 213ft (65 metres) above high water mark. It is now automatic;

Above: German memorabilia from the Occupation and Heritage Museum.

Saving the Seagulls

One of Sark's many ancient laws forbids the shooting of seagulls, because of the guidance the birds' cries gave mariners when the wind dropped and their nesting rocks and headlands vanished into sudden sea mists. Until the mid-19th century, when it was finally conceded that another war with France was unlikely, the way into Sark's harbours was a closely guarded secret.

Above: seagulls tend to live communally, in large, noisy colonies.

the platform offers superb views of Maseline Harbour and on a clear day, you can see all the way to France.

Going back to the main street, turn right into Rue Lucas to visit the

German Occupation and Heritage Museum (Easter–Sept, telephone for times on 01481-832788) on your left. The displays include old farming implements and photographs of island life, along with numerous relics of the Occupation. Sark suffered less than the other Channel Islands during the war, partly because the seigneur, Dame Sybil Hathaway, deployed her fluent German and forceful personality to ensure that island life continued along as normal a course as possible during this difficult period.

THE PRISON

Return to The Avenue, turn right, passing the shops and then left at the end of the main street. You will see, beside the **tourist information office ⑦**, a curious stone building with the prominent date of 1856: this is the two-cell **island prison**, built to hold miscreants at a time when Sark's quarrying industry – and the incidence of drunkenness and violence – were at a peak. Today the Sarkese locals take it in turn to become the Connétable (special constable) who oversees the gaol. The Connétable and his assistant, the Vingtenier, have the power to retain offenders in the gaol for two nights, after which they have to be released or transferred to Guernsey.

Below: the window-less jail can house two prisoners.

Above: La Coupée is slowly being eroded; eventually Little Sark will be an island.

Continue along the road for about a third of a mile (½km) and turn left, heading south for Little Sark.

A left turn at the next junction leads down to Stocks and Dixcart hotels, and beyond them Dixcart Bay. This is a worthwhile detour if you have time, but bear in mind that you can't get to the bay by bike. A beautiful woodland path leads to the valley bottom. You can follow the stream here on foot until it reaches the bay, a fine sandy spot for bathing when the tide is out.

LA COUPÉE

Continuing south the path bears right and the razor-edged isthmus known as **La Coupée** ❽ comes into sight. Linking the two parts of the island and looking just like a miniature stretch of the Great Wall of China, this is Sark's most famous landmark. A roadway tops this knife-edge ridge, some 10ft (3 metres) wide – too narrow for a horse and carriage but you can easily take a bike across; a notice warns cyclists to dismount while crossing. To either side there is an almost sheer drop of 260ft (80 metres) straight to the sea. Crossing La Coupée was once

extremely hazardous and schoolchildren had to crawl across the causeway in high winds, but as the plaque in the middle of the causeway relates, the path was made good with concrete and handrails in 1945 by German prisoners of war. The steep flight of steps

Above: Grand Grève beach is no longer accessible.

Ⓢ Caragh Chocolates

If you're looking for a gift from Sark, stop at Caragh Chocolates, on the left after La Coupée, coming back from Little Sark. These mouthwatering chocolates are handmade and many of them (such as 'Sark cream and double chocolate ganache' or 'Sark cream and tiramisù') contain the rich, pure (and famous) local cream. Tea gardens on the premises are open daily 10am–5pm for light lunches and cream teas with homemade cakes. There is also a pool (for a small charge) so don't forget to bring your swimming costume.

Above: Caragh chocolates make a great gift for those back home.

Above: the remains of an abandoned silver mine from the 1830s.

leading down from the north end of La Coupée to the lovely **Grand Grève** beach on the right has sadly been closed after a landslide in 2010. The cost of repair is prohibitively expensive, but on an island with so few sandy beaches, this is a great loss.

LITTLE SARK

Enjoy the views of the neighbouring islands as you follow the sunken lane to **La Sablonnerie**, a fine hotel with a restaurant and charming tea gardens, and the ivy-covered ruins of an old mill nearby. Turn left by the hotel and continue along the track until the tall granite chimneys and ruins of Sark's **silver mines** ❾, growing out of the wild bracken and brambles, come into view.

Silver was discovered on Sark in the 1830s and Cornish miners were brought over to work it. The mines produced both silver and copper, but not in sufficient quantities to be an economic success. Ten miners were drowned in 1845, and two years later, when the galleries collapsed and flooded, the ill-fated mining company went bankrupt.

Go through the gate, leave your bike and head towards the first of the chimneys, then follow the path as it bends left. Take care as these paths take you close to the cliff edge. The objective is to reach **Venus Pool** ❿, a large natural rock pool at the base of the nearby cliffs. The 10ft (3-metre) -deep pool is uncovered for 2½ hours either side of a low tide and visitors frequently fail to find it (ask locally about the tides and check the way). When the grass runs out and gives way to bare granite, cairns mark the best route. Reaching the pool involves a scramble, but you can pay homage to the goddess of love by bathing in the pool, or you can enjoy the many other smaller tide pools with their crystal-clear waters.

The gold-tinted flat rocks around it are suitable for sunbathing.

To return to La Coupée simply retrace your steps. Back on Big Sark, carry straight on along the main track, until you reach a crossroads after about half a mile (1km).

The first left leads to the **Pilcher Monument**, built to commemorate Joseph Pilcher, who drowned while crossing to Guernsey in a storm in 1868. There are fine views back to Guernsey. The right turn opposite leads down Rue de Moulin, named after the **windmill**, built by Helier de Carteret in 1571. In use until 1919, it stands at the highest point on the island, at 365ft (111 metres), and just a step away from the island's main street.

If you have time when returning to the harbour, turn right and go through the rock-cut tunnel, dug in 1588, to view Sark's original dock,

Above: the window in the rock was made to give a view of Les Autelets rocks.

pretty Creux Harbour, which was replaced by the modern port, La Maseline, in 1947.

E Eating Out

Aval du Creux Lobster Restaurant
Harbour Hill; tel: 01481-832 832, www.avalducreux.sarkislandhotels. com; lunch and dinner.
Located at the top of Harbour Hill, the Aval du Creux hotel/restaurant is well known for its fresh local seafood dishes. Meals can be served on the poolside terrace in summer. ££
Hotel Petit Champ
Tel: 01481-832 046, www.hotelpetit champ.co.uk; lunch and dinner.
On Sark's west coast, this secluded little hotel is renowned for its fresh crab and lobster dishes and organic produce from the hotel's kitchen garden. Options include light lunches by the poolside bar, cream teas, or five-course meals in the evenings. ££
La Sablonnerie
Tel: 01481-832 061; www.la sablonnerie.com; lunch and dinner, closed in winter.
Located in the south on peaceful

Little Sark this is the perfect place to stop on a walking or cycling tour. You can enjoy snacks, cream teas and seafood platters in the flower-filled tea gardens or a gourmet lunch in the restaurant, based on the ingredients produced on the hotel's organic farm. For guests at this charming old farmhouse, or others staying in Sark, there are candlelit dinners. Many consider this the best place to dine on the Channel Islands. ££
Sue's Tea Gardens
Cae de Mat; tel: 01481-832 107. Mon–Sat noon–5pm, Sun 2–5pm, closed Jan–Easter.
Sue has been running her tea gardens for many years, serving light lunches and cream teas. (This is also now a B&B). Come for fresh buttermilk scones and Sark cream, seafood chowder, mackerel pâté, home-made cakes and ice creams. Children welcome and toys are available. £

Tour 8

Alderney

Unwind on this peaceful little island caught in a time warp. The 13-mile (21km) tour, either by bike or car and foot, takes a whole day

Alderney lies just 8 miles (13km) west of Normandy, and the cobbled streets of its only town, St Anne, have a distinctly Gallic atmosphere. Some 3½ miles (5.5km) long and 1½ miles (2.5km) wide, it has cliffs to the south but to the north it slopes gently down to a series of beautiful sandy bays.

The island has largely escaped mainstream tourism and remains quiet and unspoilt, with a friendly and relaxed atmosphere and a refreshing lack of bureaucracy. It certainly feels very different from Jersey or Guernsey – it is much more sparsely populated and quite remote. There are more than 50 miles (80km) of footpaths and walks around the island, and it's a haven for bird-lovers and ornithologists.

Highlights

- St Anne
- Alderney Society Museum
- Braye
- Alderney Railway
- Mannez Lighthouse
- Burhou Island
- Les Etacs

Islanders from Guernsey and Jersey come for beaches, golf, quirky shops and – last but not least – the restaurants and watering holes. The islanders have a reputation for conviviality and there is a definite emphasis on taking time out to eat, drink and be merry. If you're tired of walking Alderney's wind-blasted cliffs in a squall, sitting in a warm pub is the best thing to do. The pubs are more like clubs – full of character and characters, and the natural place to be on an island that offers few places of entertainment. Alderney stole a march on Guernsey by being the first to allow publicans to open on Sundays.

Alderney's character differs somewhat from the other islands, partly because it was deliberately depopulated during World War II and used as a forced labour camp. The island was massively fortified by the Germans; relics of the Occupation can be seen along the coastline.

Alderney is small enough to feel like an island, with the sea nearly always in view, yet large enough for day-trippers to leave feeling that they could have done with a little more time. If you decide to stay overnight there are several hotels and guesthouses.

This day tour of the island can be covered either entirely by bike, or by a combination of car and foot. If time is limited there are regular bus tours of the island, available on certain days, or taxis that offer affordable tours.

Above: a German watchtower.
Left: a shopping street in St Anne.

GETTING TO ALDERNEY

From Guernsey the easiest way to get to Alderney is to hop across by plane. If you're accustomed to bargain-basement flights this is a journey of a lifetime. You'll travel in one of the tiny Trislanders, the pilot welcomes you in person and everyone has a window seat with wonderful views. Look closely and you can almost see the

Capital Shopping

The shops in St Anne are delightfully quirky. No high street stores or Starbucks here, but family butchers and bakers, shops selling fishing tackle, bric-a-brac and sweets in old-fashioned large glass jars. As in France, all the shops close down for a two hour lunch break. If you're feeling the breeze, walk down to Channel Jumpers in Braye Street where you can buy traditional Guernsey and Alderney sweaters.

Above: an old-fashioned greengrocer's shop in St Anne.

lobster pots. Alderney Airport was the first officially recognised airport of the Channel Islands, opened in 1935, and still not much more than a few prefab huts and a hangar. Going by sea (www.bumblebee.gg) is a cheaper option, but the boat takes an hour as opposed to a 15-minute flight.

For the energetic visitor, hiring a bike is a good way of seeing the island (Cycle & Surf, St Anne, tel: 01481-822 286 or Auto Motion, Braye Harbour, tel: 01481-823 352). You can't cover the entire island in a day on foot, but there are some wonderful walks and distances between the main landmarks are easily walkable. Taxis will be wait-

Above: a plaque in Victoria Street commemorates the monarch's visit.

ing at the airport for round-the-island tours (ABC Taxis, tel: 01381-823 760, Island Taxis, tel: 01481-823 823). ABC Taxis operate very reasonably priced two-hour tours of the island departing at 2pm from the bottom of Victoria Street, St Anne, on Tuesday, Wednesday and Thursday. You can also hire a car (Braye Hire Cars, tel: 01481-823 881; www.brayehirecars.com). Driving couldn't be easier: no traffic lights, no road rage and not much traffic.

ST ANNE

The capital, **St Anne** ❶ (referred to by locals simply as 'town') is an attractive maze of cobbled streets lined by houses of granite and sandstone, many of them whitewashed or painted in lovely pastel shades. **Victoria Street**, named after the monarch who visited Alderney on 9 August 1854, has most of Alderney's shops and restaurants. It's worth popping into the **Alderney Visitor and Wildlife Information Centre** for some excellent walking guides.

Just south of the information centre is the entrance to **St Anne's Church**. This massive French-style building of local granite, with Caen stone details, was designed by Sir George Gilbert

Above: St Anne's Church on Alderney is often referred to as the Cathedral of the Channel Islands.

ALDERNEY SOCIETY MUSEUM

The tower and churchyard stand near the **Alderney Society Museum** (Easter–Oct Mon–Fri 10am–noon and 2.30–4.30pm, Sat–Sun 10am–noon; charge), which is housed in the former Old School, founded in 1790 by the island's governor, Jean Le Mesurier. The museum provides a detailed account of the island, from its geology and wildlife to such topics as whether the Alderney cow ever existed as a distinct breed.

One section deals with wartime Occupation and the evacuation of all but a handful of the island's population. From 1942–4 Alderney was used as a forced labour camp with almost 5,000 labourers from all over Europe transported here to turn the island into an impregnable fortress. The labourers toiled in harsh conditions; several hundred of them died from starvation and brutality. Alderney had the only concentration camp on British soil during the war, with 1,000 inmates from Sachsenhausen concentration camp transported here to work on fortifications.

Scott in 'chaste Gothic' style, and opened in 1850. It replaced the old church, which was described at the time as 'small and mean'. The body of the **Old Church** was demolished, but you will find the squat tower, which survived, and the old churchyard, containing some fine 18th-century tombstones, by continuing to the top of Victoria Street and then turning right into the High Street.

Above: cannon found in an Elizabethan wreck, Alderney Society Museum.

When the Alderney residents were allowed to return in the winter of 1945, they had to agree to work cooperatively, under central management, to restore houses and farmland left derelict by the occupying forces. Hard work and self-sacrifice saw the island economy restored within two years, but there were moments of farce, as illustrated by the infamous Battle of the Butes. This took place in 1945 after British troops, preparing for the islanders' return, cleaned out their homes and stacked such furniture as had survived in the open air, with a rope barrier. A free-for-all broke loose once the rope was removed, with islanders fighting each other for their possessions. For decades after, it is said, some people on the island refused to invite others into their homes for fear that their guest might recognise a family heirloom.

Another section of the museum displays artefacts salvaged from the Elizabethan warship, the 60ft (18-metre) *Makeshift*, wrecked off the coast of Alderney and discovered in 1977 by a fisherman. Apart from a cannon, pottery and leather clothing, two of the most intriguing finds are early tobacco pipes – one made of pottery and one

of pewter – with tiny bowls, reflecting the fact that tobacco, introduced to Europe only two decades previously, was still a very expensive luxury.

ISLAND HALL

Close to the museum are some of Alderney's oldest buildings: turning right just beyond the museum will take you into Connaught Square, with the Old Government House of 1763, now better known as **Island Hall** where States of Alderney, the island parliament, used to hold its meetings. It is now the seat of the States' civil service department. The imposing Georgian building was originally constructed as a private house for the Le Mesuriers, the hereditary governors of Alderney, who clawed their way to wealth and status through acts of licensed piracy. In one year alone during the wars with France, Jean Le Mesurier, under a licence granted by the English Crown, captured shipping valued at £135,000 – a fortune in the late 18th century.

BRAYE

From the centre of St Anne it's just a few minutes' walk down the hill to Braye Harbour. The great sandy

Above: Island Hall, where Alderney parliament used to hold its meetings.

Above: Braye Harbour has one of the longest harbour walls in Europe.

sweep of Braye beach is protected by the Alderney breakwater and therefore offers sheltered bathing. The harbour is safe from the strong current of the Swinge, just off-shore. For all its small size, Braye has more than its fair share of places to eat, from chip shops and pubs to up-market seafood restaurants.

THE BRAYE BREAKWATER

Along with Alderney's ring of 12 defensive fortifications, the **Braye Breakwater ❷** is a legacy of the suspicion that existed between England and France in the early 19th century, even though hostilities officially ceased after the defeat of Napoleon. When the French began constructing a naval harbour at Cherbourg, alarm bells rang in the Admiralty, and the British government suddenly decided it was urgent to build 'harbours of refuge' at Braye on Alderney, as well as on Guernsey and Jersey. The intention

Ⓖ The Alderney Spike Girls

Only on Alderney are you ever likely to see a blonde hedgehog. These creamy-coloured flea-free creatures, with beady button-black eyes, have a rare recessive gene. There is a population of around 1,000 on the island and they have been breeding here since a couple of them were released in the 1960s – allegedly from a Harrods shopping bag. You are most likely to see them at dusk or in the early morning.

Above: the blonde hedgehog is not an albino, it has a recessive gene.

Ⓕ Cricketing Ties

Alderney has strong links with well-known cricketing characters. John Arlott, once His Master's Voice of BBC cricket commentaries, retired to Alderney in 1981 saying it was a 'desperately easy place' to live in with a 'pleasant absence of bores'. Ian Botham was a regular player here and had a holiday home on the island. Since the 19th century cricket has been played on Les Butes, a spectacular pitch with sea views.

Above: visiting teams tend to stay for Saturday only, playing a shortened version of the game.

was to convert Braye harbour into a massive naval base, with a breakwater at each side of the bay. Only the western wall was built, completed in 1847 and originally a mile (½km) long. Battered by massive waves (signs warn walkers that the wall is liable to sudden swamping by breaking waves), part of the breakwater was abandoned and now lies submerged beneath the waves, a hazard to shipping.

Today local fishermen cast their lines from the breakwater, and during winter storms locals congregate here to watch the waves crash dramatically against the wall.

THE ALDERNEY RAILWAY

The **Alderney Railway** ❸, one of the oldest in the British Isles, was constructed in the 1840s by the British government to convey stone from Mannez Quarry to build the breakwater and the forts. The first official passengers were Queen Victoria and Prince Albert, who were carried in 1854 in a horse-drawn tender.

At weekends and on bank holidays from Easter to September, the railway carries passengers on a 2-mile (3km) trip from the harbour up to the northeast coast, a journey of 15 minutes (departures at 2.30pm and 3.30pm on Sun in May–June, Sat and Sun in July, Sun in September; for information tel: 01481-822 978 or visit www.alderney railway.com). Passengers are either carried in a diesel-powered railcar, or in one of two 1938 London Underground carriages. The bright red tube carriages shuttling beneath the gorse- and bracken-covered hills of Longis Common make a bizarre sight.

THE NORTHEAST COAST

A circular road hugs the northeastern coast, forming a loop from Braye back

Above: an abandoned rail line along the Braye harbour breakwater.

Above: Fort Albert affords wonderful views of the marine life in Braye harbour.

to St Anne. Following the Lower Road east out of Braye, you will skirt Braye Bay and encounter **Fort Albert** ❹, the first in the chain of 12 fortresses encircling the island, designed in the 1840s and 1850s. Suspicious of French intentions, the English imported hundreds of English and Irish labourers to construct these fine fortifications of pink granite, but most were never subsequently garrisoned. Several have now been converted into private flats and holiday apartments, while others remain in a decayed and dangerous state – best appreciated from afar. Fort Albert is perhaps the finest of them all, and is well positioned to defend Braye Harbour.

HAMMOND MEMORIAL

A short way on, the road divides; the spot is marked by the **Hammond Memorial** ❺ commemorating the many prisoners of war who died on Alderney during the Occupation period. They were imported to work as slave labourers on the construction of the defences that were to turn the Channel Islands into the most heavily fortified area in Europe. Plaques in Hebrew, Polish, Russian and Span-

ish indicate the origins of those who lost their lives: Spanish partisans who were on the losing side in the Civil War, Jews from Alsace and Czecho-slovakia, and prisoners of war from Russia and Poland.

SAYE AND CORBLETS BAYS

Fork left at the memorial for **Saye Bay** (pronounced 'Soy'), an idyllic horseshoe-shaped white-sand beach

Above: Corblets Bay offers excellent swimming and surfing.

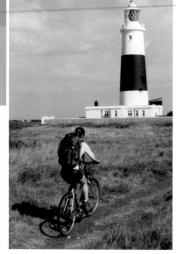

Above: the Mannez Lighthouse beam is visible 23 miles (37km) out to sea.

between rocky headlands. Children love leaping off the rocks here – and in summer it's popular with campers from the island's only campsite just over the dunes. The next beach along is the delightful **Corblets Bay**, with clean sands and shallow waters. This is the best beach on the island for surfing and bodyboarding.

MANNEZ QUARRY AND LIGHTHOUSE

Evidence of quarrying activity lies all around the northeastern tip of the island at **Mannez Quarry**, close to the railway station terminus. Above the quarry stands the large and sinister fire control tower, built by the Germans to act as a command post for the various artillery batteries around the island. It is known locally as The Odeon. From here there are clear views across to the Cap de la Hague in Normandy. Mannez Pond at the eastern end of the quarry provides a rich habitat for wetland birds as well as Alderney's nine species of dragonflies. **Mannez Lighthouse** ❻ (closed indefinitely to visitors) is Al-

derney's most conspicuous landmark. It was built in 1912 to aid vessels along this treacherous stretch of coast.

LONGIS BAY

Continuing round the coast, another fine stretch of sandy beach is found at **Longis Bay** ❼. Additional shelter is provided by the massive concrete anti-tank wall. This was partially constructed by the Germans, who were convinced that the Allies would eventually try to retake the Channel Islands by landing tanks and troops. The structure remains incomplete. At the far end of Longis Bay, an attractive château-like building, known locally as **The Nunnery**, stands on the site of Alderney's Roman fort. It was here that the coins, pottery and bronze work in Alderney Museum were excavated, while much of the museum's Iron-Age material came from a site on the adjacent golf course. Just to the north, **Longis Pond** has a bird-hide, information point and bird feeding area, perfect for ornithologists.

HANGING ROCKS

The Nunnery marks the point at which Alderney's lowlands give out. Just to the south, the cliffs rise steeply

Above: Longis Bay features an uncompleted tank wall and sandy beaches.

Ⓖ Puffin Webcam

The Alderney Wildlife Trust's puffin webcam (www.alderneywildlife.org) streams live footage of puffins on the island of Burhou. The best time to check out the puffins is during the afternoon and early evening. From June onwards you may see adults returning with fish and sand eels for their growing chicks. The site also features a puffin forum and information on the birds and their habitats.

Above: puffins are often called 'sea parrots' due to their colourful beaks.

to the landmark known as the **Hanging Rocks**. Here, two huge boulders look as if they have detached themselves from the cliff and are about to tumble into the sea. One local legend has it that Jerseymen, jealous of Alderney's beauty, once tried to tow the island closer to their own by attaching a rope to the rocks; all they succeeded in doing was to tilt the rocks. **Essex Castle**, now private flats, stands high above the rocks, while the main road leads straight uphill, back to St Anne.

SOUTH OF THE ISLAND

The southern part of the island can only properly be explored on foot or by bike, since the best parts of the coast are only accessible by paths. Allow a couple of hours for this 5-mile (8km) exploration of the southern cliffs and take binoculars for spectacular views of gannetries.

If you are coming from St Anne, start at the church and take the western exit from the churchyard. Turn right to follow the road called La Vallée down to the sea at Saline Bay. Turn left to follow the coast road, past **Fort Tourgis**, derelict for 30 years.

Take the road to the right of the fort to follow the coast. The surfaced road soon gives way to a track, leading to **Fort Clonque** ❽, built

in 1854 and sited on an offshore islet. The fort has been converted to holiday apartments by the Landmark Trust *(see page 126)*. You can only access the fort when the tide is out, as the causeway is covered by water at high tide. The intertidal rocks at Clonque Bay are perfect for rock pooling. At the northern end, the wreck of the SS *Emily Eveson* reveals itself at low tide. You can then walk

Above: Fort Clonque stands on its own rocky island.

The islands lying offshore are called Les Etacs (also known as Garden Rocks). What looks like snow covering these rocky islets is, in fact, a colony of gannets, which first arrived on the rocks in 1939. The colony expanded rapidly during the war. Now about 7,000 pairs nest here from spring, departing again every autumn. Les Etacs and nearby Ortac rocks support more than 2 percent of the world's gannet population. From the southern coast you can also see the islands of Sark, with Brecqhou to the right, then Herm and Guernsey.

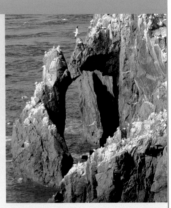

Above: the gannet is a protected species in the United Kingdom.

out and look inside its boiler, but beware of the tides.

BURHOU ISLAND

From Fort Clonque you can see across to the tiny uninhabited **island of Burhou** ❾. With no rats, no cats and very little human disturbance, the island is a haven for breeding sea birds, including more than 120 breeding pairs of puffins. In 2005 the island and surrounding wetlands were granted Ramsar status *(see page 59)* to protect the birdlife and marine species.

Burhou has a closed season from mid-March to 1 August but there are 2½-hour boat trips on certain days in summer, to view the puffin and gannet colonies on Burhou Island, Ortac and Les Etacs and the Atlantic seal colony near Burhou Reef. You might even spot the odd basking shark in summer. For information on boat trips go to www.visitalderney.com.

SOUTH COAST CLIFFS

This is Alderney at its most beautiful and ruggedly spectacular. Follow the track known as **'The ZigZag'**, as it

winds uphill, and enjoy the amazing views. Turn left at the next junction, then right onto a surfaced track, which turns back into a rough track after a short distance. Continue to the view-

Above: there were once steps down to Telegraph Bay, but the way is now too treacherous for it to remain open.

ing point at the end of the headland, above **Trois Vaux Bay**.

TELEGRAPH BAY

Retrace your steps and take the next turn right. Ignore the next right, but take the right turn after that to head for Telegraph Bay. This was previously a favourite retreat for swimming and sunbathing if the tide was out, but since the steps fell into disrepair the beach has sadly been inaccessible. The bay is named after the Telegraph Tower that stands atop the headland, used in the early 19th century to send semaphore signals to the other islands.

Admire the views from the bench at the top of the bay, then return to the main track and turn right, skirting the southern side of the airport. The track bends northwards at the far side of the airfield, taking you, via La Petite Rue, back to St Anne's High Street and the centre of town.

Eating Out

St Anne
Bumps Eating House
Braye Street, St Anne; tel: 01481-823 197; dinner only except on Sun and in high season, closed Wed.
The chef of this excellent eatery is also the owner, which is always good news. Vegetarian options feature on the menu alongside steaks and superb seafood. Friday night is fish night with a 3- or 4-course fixed price menu. ££
Georgian House
Victoria Street, St Anne; tel: 01481-822 471; www.georgianalderney.com; lunch and dinner.
The best place to eat at this restaurant is in the lovely sheltered garden at the rear of the hotel. The menu is a mix of traditional English pub and European cuisine, with emphasis on seafood, and use of local and sustainable produce where possible. Very friendly staff. ££
Gloria's Food
Olliver Street, St Anne; tel: 01481-822 500; breakfast, lunch and dinner.
This is a firm favourite thanks to Gloria's creative home-made meals, generous portions and relaxed, welcoming atmosphere. Think freshly cooked tapas, Morrocan lamb tagine and Cajun chicken. Be sure to reserve a table if going on a Friday or Saturday evening due to this place's popularity. £–££

Jack's Brasserie
Victoria Street, tel: 01481-823 933; daily 9am–10pm.
This is a popular spot for breakfasts, light lunches and coffee and cakes. With a sunny terrace on the High Street, it's a good spot to relax and watch the world go by. £

Braye
Braye Beach Hotel Restaurant
Braye Street, tel: 01481-824 300, www.brayebeach.com; lunch and dinner.
Book a table overlooking the lovely Braye beach and tuck into turbot with pan-seared scallops, shellfish bisque or butter-poached lobster. The hotel is rated 4-star so prices are higher than average but the £25 set menu is good value. ££–£££
Braye Chippie
Braye Harbour, tel: 01481-823 475; Wed–Sat 5.30–9pm, longer hours in high season.
Very popular, with plenty of seating inside and out, right by the harbour. Bring your own bottle. £
First and Last
Braye Harbour, tel: 01481-823 162; closed Tue lunch.
Rita is a great hostess and produces some of the best seafood dishes in the Channel Islands. Expect freshly caught lobster, scallops and crab as well as steak, poultry and home-made desserts. Has harbour views. ££

Travel Tips

Active Pursuits

From golf and guided walks to coasteering and kayaking, the island of Guernsey has plenty of outdoor sports and activities to keep you occupied.

With 28 miles (45km) of stunning cliff-top paths, beautiful bays for water sports and clear blue seas for fishing, there is no shortage of ways to enjoy the great outdoors. Along with long-established activities such as golf and sailing, sports enthusiasts can now try out abseiling, coasteering and other adventure activities. For full details go to www.visitguernsey.com (click on Activities).

WALKING

Walking opportunities are plentiful, from dramatic rugged cliffs to the leafy lanes of the interior. The most spectacular and challenging walk is the south coast footpath, which dips down to villages where you can take a break at beachside cafés. The walk can either be done in its entirety over a long day, or in separate shorter sections at a gentler pace. The scenery is best in spring when wild flowers are in bloom and birds come ashore to nest.

An extensive programme of themed walks with accredited guides runs from April to September. Information is available from the Guernsey Information Centre, which also provides a series of trail leaflets and a free walking map of Guernsey.

During the Spring and Autumn Walking Weeks, guided walks focus on different aspects of Guernsey's natural beauty and heritage, with around 40 walks to choose from. *Walking on Guernsey* by Cicerone Guides (£12.95) is an excellent booklet describing 24 walks on Guernsey, Alderney, Sark and Herm. The most detailed maps of the islands are the Ordnance Survey-style Bailiwick of Guernsey (1:15,000) or the Perry's official guide. When exploring the coast, watch out for extreme tidal movement, one of the largest recorded in the world. Beaches can disappear rapidly, so it's best to plan with an abundance of caution. And don't forget comfortable shoes, binoculars and sunblock.

Alderney has 50 miles (80km) of footpaths, across commons, cliffs and beaches. The Alderney Wildlife Trust organises informative guided walks throughout the year, ranging from history and heritage to birdwatching and bat walks, plus useful leaflets on self-guided walks. During Alderney Wildlife Week in May guided walks explore the wide range of habitat and species on the island, including the unusual blonde hedgehogs. The small island of Sark is ideal for walking, as is its neighbouring island Herm, although there you have no other choice.

The Channel Island Way is an exciting new 110-mile walking route incorporating the best coastal walks in Jersey, Guernsey, Alderney, Sark and Herm. With a bit of island hopping (by boat or plane) ramblers can discover

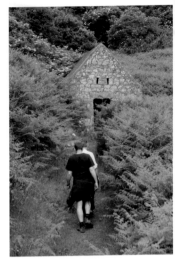

Previous Pages: Castle Cornet in St Peter Port. **Left**: parasailing. **Above**: hiking through lush vegetation.

one of the most beautiful and diverse walking destinations in the UK. Serious ramblers can do the whole route in the space of a fortnight (including the island-hops on ferries or boats). Obviously you don't have to do the

Ⓚ Fishing for Razor Clams

When the tide is low children can have fun trying to catch razor fish (also known as razor clams). Go equipped with a bag of salt, walk along the shoreline and look for the keyhole-shaped burrows in the sand. Sprinkle a teaspoon of salt over the hole, wait for the clam to pop out of its burrow, then pull it gently out of the hole. The clams are slightly chewy but can be delicious if cooked correctly, ideally steamed with wine, garlic and herbs. The best beaches for collecting the clams are L'Ancresse Bay and any of the west coast beaches on a low spring tide.

Above: razor fish or clams have a fragile, curved shell.

ⓕ One Toe in the Sea

If you are used to indoor pools or swimming in the Mediterranean, the Channel Island waters will feel on the cool side. In the summer months temperatures average around 63°F (17°C). This means that most beachgoers do no more than paddle, leaving the seas delightfully crowd-free for serious swimmers. The beaches are washed twice daily by the tides and the waters are clear, but beware of strong currents and rip tides.

Above: paddling in the cool waters along the beach in Guernsey.

whole route, nor do you have to be a super-fit walker. The routes on the main islands are divided into sections of 2–4 miles, with a car park, bus stop and café at each end. *The Channel Island Way* guide is published by Coast Media (£9.95) and is packed with practical information as well as points of interest and local history.

ANGLING

With their varied coastlines, offshore reefs and clear waters the Channel Islands are ideal locations for sea

Above: cyclists cross La Coupée to Little Sark.

anglers, especially from mid-summer to the end of autumn. Around 70 different species of fish are caught from the shores, including conger, rays, turbot, bass and bream. No permission is needed to fish from the coastline or harbours. A number of commercial operators offer fishing trips. Angling boat trips include *Out the Blue II* charters (www.boatfishing.net) for groups of 10–12 with a choice of wreck fishing, deep sea reef fishing, bank fishing or bass angling. For tailor-made fishing packages, including Herm shore fishing trips, contact John Rothwell at www.guernseyfishingguide.com.

Alderney is one of the best places in the British Isles for shore fishing with a large range of species, including turbot, mullet, ling, tope, bass, bream, plaice, sole and thick-lipped mullet. St Anne has a well-stocked tackle and bait shop which can organise lessons for the novice or young angler.

CYCLING

The tourist board VisitGuernsey publishes an excellent free guide to way-marked cycle paths called *Guernsey Cycle Tours: 11 Island Routes*. Routes are graded from 'Gentle & Rolling' to the more arduous 'Up Hill and Down Dale' and are designed to take in the island's tourist attractions as well as refreshment stops. No distance on Guernsey is too far to cycle, though you may find the amount of traffic you encounter both on inland and coastal roads offputting. The most pleasant roads are the *Ruettes Tranquilles* (Quiet Lanes) where pedestrians, cyclists and horse-riders have priority over cars, and motorists are meant to slow down to a sedate 15mph (24kmh). Cycling is an ideal way of getting around car-free Sark *(see Tour 7, page 82)*. For cycle hire in Guernsey see page 117.

WATERSPORTS

Sailing and Windsurfing

For sailing or windsurfing lessons contact the Guernsey Sailing Trust, (tel: 01481-710 877; www.sailingtrust.org. gg). The waters are popular among yachting enthusiasts but inexperienced sailors should beware of the tides and currents. Skippered boat charter can be organised through Guernsey Boating (www.guernseyboating.com).

Surfing and Scuba Diving

The rollers on Guernsey are not comparable to those on Jersey, but you can find surf on the island's west coast and on Alderney. The Guernsey Surf School at Vazon (tel: 07911 710 789; www.guernseysurfschool.co.uk) offers lessons and courses.

Conditions are good for scuba diving with clean (and cold) waters, good visibility and plentiful marine life. The Blue Dolphins Sub Aqua Club (tel: 01481-712 492; www.bd sac.org.gg), a branch of the British Sub Aqua Club, offers a range of diving experiences, including shipwrecks. Dive Sark (tel: 01481-832 565; www. sarkci.com) organises courses and dives to explore the reefs and caves around the island; book early to avoid

Below: sea kayaking is available on Cobo Bay for experienced adults.

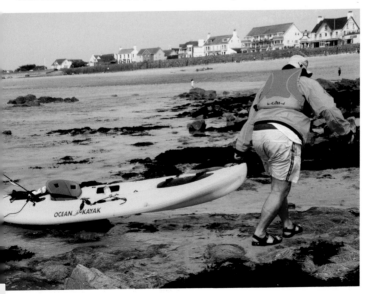

disappointment. The clear waters around the islands are also excellent for snorkelling and swimming.

ADVENTURE SPORTS

You can abseil on the west coast as the sun sets, climb the cliffs in the morning light, or roll down the hill inside a giant transparent plastic ball (zorbing). Coasteering routes enable punters to experience the exhilaration of sea-level traversing, rock scrambling, kayaking, jumping and swimming in gullies and caves. You just come equipped with a swimming costume, a good pair of trainers, shorts or tracksuit, and a change of clothes for later. For further information visit www.outdoorguernsey.co.uk or call 01481-267 627.

GOLF

Guernsey has two 18-hole courses. The number one is the Royal Guernsey at L'Ancresse (tel: 01481-246 523; www.royalguernseygolfclub.com) in the north of the island, where visitors need to produce a handicap certificate from a recognised club. La Grande Mare at Vazon Bay, Castel (tel: 01481-253 432; www.lagrandemare.com) is a hotel-based course. There is also a 9-hole par 3 course designed by Tony Jacklin at St Pierre Park Hotel, St Peter Port (tel: 01481-727 739; www.stpierrepark.co.uk).

On Alderney the 9-hole Alderney Golf Club (tel: 01481-822 835; www.alderneygolfclub.com) is a scenic and testing course, with fine views of France.

HEALTH AND LEISURE

Keep in shape at King's Life Health and Leisure Club on King's Road, St Peter Port (tel: 01481-723 366; www.kings-life.com), with all the latest fitness equipment. The club has indoor and outdoor swimming pools, spa, sauna and steam rooms, six tennis

Below: golf course with Napoleonic towers at L'Ancresse Common.

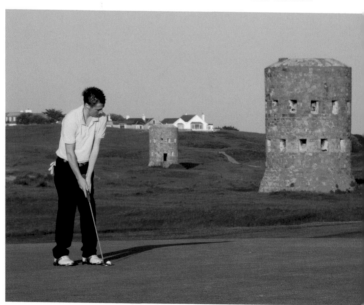

F Boat Trips

Cruising around the Guernsey coast, chartering a speed boat, spotting dolphins or seals, landing mackerel or sea bass, hopping across to Herm or Sark and taking a ferry to France are among the many boating options. To see the wildlife around Guernsey, the smaller islands and offshore reefs, take a trip in a rigid inflatable boat (Rib Voyages, www.islandribvoyages.com). On Sark a boat trip is the best way to explore the rugged coast, caves and birdlife, and on Alderney to see the puffin colony and gannetries.

Above: visitors often enjoy a ferry trip to take in the wildlife.

courts, four squash courts, a gym with studio classes, a bar and restaurant. Day memberships are available.

The Beau Séjour Leisure Centre, Amherst, St Peter Port (tel: 01481-747 200 for sports bookings) is the place to take the family on rainy days *(see page 28)*.

HORSE RIDING

Treks and escorted hacks along bridle paths normally last two or three hours. The long-established Melrose Farm Riding School (Castel parish, Guernsey; tel: 01481-252 151) is approved by the British Horse Society (a sign of quality) and caters for all ages and standards. It has an all-weather arena overlooking the west coast and takes rides onto Vazon beach.

On Alderney you can explore scenic cliffs and country paths on horseback, and from October to March, on the beaches too. To book a ride call Jill Moore (tel: 07781-421 325).

Late August sees the annual Alderney Horse Show, with showjumping and showing classes sharing the schedule with equine fancy dress and dog agility classes. This family-friendly show is open to all.

Below: horse riding on the beach is a romantic way to see the scenery.

Themed Holidays

Themed holidays on Guernsey run the range from eco-camping to gourmet weekends.

WILD FOOD FORAGING WORKSHOPS AND ECO-CAMPING

Wild Guernsey offers half-day workshops for very small groups focusing on food foraged from hedgerows, fields and seashore. Learn about sustainability, work in the wild and sample seaweed or rock samphire from the shore, pennywort (like mangetout) from the hedgerows or wild onions from the waysides. The workshops sit alongside Green Tourism Gold awarded sustainable camping (luxury canvas tipi or bell tent) overlooking the Bay of Rocquaine on the west coast, just one minute from the beach. Wild swimming, kayaking, snorkelling, surfing, guided walking and cycling can also be arranged. For details call Tara de Jersey, tel: 07781122420 or 07781131711 or email: wildguernsey@yahoo.co.uk.

SUMMER CAMPS

Young surfers can join non-residential summer camps with the Guernsey Surf School (tel: 07911710789; www.guernseysurfschool.co.uk). Apart from surf tuition, there is rock-jumping, beach games, kayaking, snorkelling and board design. Courses take place from July to September for 8–16 year olds.

FISHING HOLIDAYS

John Rothwell, who holds the garfish shore record, organises tailor-made fishing trips all year round on Guernsey, Sark and Herm. He will arrange accommodation – anything from a campsite to 4-star luxury. Expect to catch bass, ballam wrasse, grey mullet, black bream and more. (Information at www.guernseyfishingguide.com; tel: 07781441012.)

THE WHITE HOUSE WEEKENDS, HERM

The White House Hotel (tel: 01481-750 075; www.herm.com) offers themed weekend packages from Guernsey, typically wine tasting and gourmet weekends. Packages include transport from Guernsey as well as accommodation.

LUXURY SPA BREAKS

For a spell of relaxation and rejuvenation try a spa break at the Old Government House Hotel (see page 125) or the St Pierre Park (www.stpierre park.co.uk). For details contact Fly Guernsey (www.flyguernsey.com; tel: 0845-2303240).

YOGA RETREATS

De-stress and reconnect with yourself and others in a tranquil setting. Reiki, massage and reflexology on offer. For retreat information go to www.be inspiredby.co.uk.

Above: Guernsey's west coast and Alderney offer some great waves for surfing.

Practical Information

GETTING THERE

Year-round air and sea packages, short breaks, flights and accommodation can all be arranged through specialist tour operators. For details see www.visitguernsey.com/tour-operators.

By air

All visitors flying to the Channel Islands need a passport or photo ID. Regular year-round flights operate from airports throughout the UK (but not Heathrow) with added flights in high season. Flights take 40 minutes from London Gatwick and as little as 30 minutes from some regional airports. **Flybe** (tel: 0871-700 2000; www.flybe.com) flies direct to Guernsey from Birmingham, Newcastle, Norwich, Southampton, Exeter, Edinburgh, Glasgow, Dublin and Belfast City, while **easyJet** (www.easyjet.com) is starting a new direct service from Gatwick to Guernsey in 2014. The Guernsey airline **Aurigny** (tel: 01481-822 886; www.aurigny.com) flies from London Gatwick, London Stansted, Manchester, East Midlands, Bristol and Southampton. **Blue Islands** (tel: 0845-620 2122; www.blueislands.com) operates direct flights from Southampton, and connecting routes (via Jersey) from London City, Bristol and Isle of Man. The best prices are normally secured by booking well in advance on the internet and avoiding weekends and the busiest times of year. Both Aurigny and Blue Islands provide a Channel Island hopping service between Jersey, Alderney and Guernsey.

By sea

The only ferry line from the UK to Jersey is Condor Ferries (tel: 0845-609 1026; www.condorferries.co.uk) which operates high-speed catamaran services from Weymouth to Guernsey all year round (2 hours 30 mins) and from Poole from May to September (3 hours). Ferries take cars as well as passengers, and provide a cafeteria, TV room for children and duty-free shop

Below: Aurigny is the Norman name for Alderney, as well as for the local airline.

Above: local buses trundle around Guernsey.

with some excellent deals, especially on alcohol. Club-class seating is available, with reclining seats and complementary refreshments.

Condor also operates a slower ferry service from Portsmouth on the conventional Clipper ferry. The return crossing is overnight with the option of 1-, 2-, 3- or 4-berth cabins and en suite facilities. From Guernsey, it is a 20-minute ferry hop to Herm and 45 minutes to Sark; Jersey and Alderney are each a 15-minute flight away, or one hour by sea.

Visitors bringing their own car must have an insurance certificate or an International Green Card, the complete vehicle registration document and a valid driving licence or International Driving Permit. Bikes can be taken across on the Condor ferries free of charge.

GETTING AROUND

Guernsey has a variety of transport options, both public and private. The smaller islands, however, leave you with little choice between a bicycle and your own feet.

Buses

Guernsey has a new network of scheduled bus services. All the bus numbers have changed and the flat fare, applying to all journeys of any distance, has doubled for tourists from £1 to £2. Travel passes are available for 1, 2 and 7 days for individuals and families. The new network has 11 routes, servicing most parts of the island and all of the major attractions. Timetables and maps are available from the bus terminal, Visitor Information Centre or online at www.hctgroup.org. Double check the times as the new timetables are subject to alterations.

Several companies operate scheduled or tailor-made bus tours, including Island Coachways (tel: 01481-720 210, www.icw.gg) and Intransit (tel: 01481-700 066; www.intransitlimited.com).

Car hire

Car hire prices are among the cheapest in western Europe, and fuel tends to be slightly cheaper than the UK price. Child seats and cars with automatic transmission cost extra. Drivers must have held a full licence for a year and must be over 20 or 21 years of age (depending on the company). There are also varying maximum age restrictions. Car hire companies in Guernsey include Avis (tel: 0844 581 0147, outside the UK: +44 844 544 5566), Europcar (tel: 01481-239 511; www.europcarguernsey.com) and Hertz (tel: 0800 735 1014; www.hertz ci.com). On Alderney, try Braye Hire cars (tel: 01481-823 881, www.braye hirecars.com).

Driving

The rules of the road are the same as those in the UK: driving is on the left, seat belts are compulsory and it is an offence to use a mobile phone whilst driving. Fixed alcohol limits and roadside breath testing are similar to the UK.

The maximum speed limit is 35mph (55kph) and less in many areas. In towns it is 25mph (40kph) and on the *Ruettes Tranquilles* (Quiet Lanes) motorists must slow down to 15mph (24kmh). A yellow line across the junction of a minor road means stop and give way to traffic on the major road. A yellow arrow on the road warns of a junction ahead. Many junctions on Guernsey have a filter-in-turn system, marked by a cross-hatched yellow box painted on the road. You must not enter the box until your exit is clear.

Most roads are very narrow, visibility can be poor at junctions, and the lanes are used by tractors, cyclists, pedestrians and horses, as well as buses and cars, so be aware of your surroundings.

Parking often requires a 'parking clock' which can be purchased from the Guernsey Information Centre, Airport Information Desk, police station and from some garages and newsagents.

Cycling

(See also under Active Pursuits, *page 110.*) Bikes can be hired from Millard & Co, 9–11 Victoria Street, St Peter Port (tel: 01481-720 777; www. millards.org) or Guernsey Cycle Hire, North Plantation, St Peter Port (tel: 07781-192 033; www.guernseyhire. co.uk).

Cycle hire shops are plentiful on Alderney (by the harbour in Braye, and in Victoria Street) and on Sark (at the top of Harbour Hill and along The Avenue).

Inter-island ferries and France

Herm: Travel Trident (tel: 01481-721 379; www.traveltrident.com) operates ferries from St Peter Port to Herm roughly every hour in summer, with fewer boats in the off-peak season. Go early to avoid the day-trippers in the summer. The booking office is on the corner of North Esplanade and St Julian's Pier.

Sark: The Isle of Sark Shipping Company (tel: 01481-724 059; www. sarkshippingcompany.com) runs day trips to Sark with five ferries a day in summer.

Above: rent a bicycle to best experience the island of Sark.

Alderney: the fastest, though certainly not the cheapest, way to visit the smaller island of Alderney from Guernsey is to take the 15-minute flight operated by Aurigny or Blue Islands *(see page 115)*.

Day trips to Jersey and France: Condor Ferries (www.condorferries.co.uk) operates day trips from St Peter Port to Jersey, and to St-Malo in France. Manche Îles Express (tel: 01481-701 316; www.manche-iles.com) operates ferries connecting Guernsey with Jersey, and Carteret, Diélette and Granville in Normandy (both take 60 minutes).

Taxis

Guernsey has licensed taxis at two ranks in central St Peter Port, one at St Sampson's and another at the airport. Pre-booking is advisable whenever possible. Taxi companies include:

A+S Taxis, tel: 07781-125 544; Island Taxis, tel: 01481-700 500; Panza Taxis, tel: 07781 111340.

FACTS FOR THE VISITOR

Disabled Travellers

For information for disabled travellers in Guernsey, go to www.disabledgo.com/en/org/guernsey-1. The Radar National Key Scheme, which enables disabled people to access locked public toilets, operates in Guernsey. Visitors are advised to bring their own key; alternatively they are available from the Guernsey Information Centre.

On-street parking and public car parks have designated areas for UK and European Blue Badge holders. Guernsey buses are accessible for all wheelchairs apart from those over 29ins (75cm) wide, or a wheelchair and occupant weighing a total of more than 660lbs (300kg).

Below: the Condor Ferry departs from St Peter Port, bound for the mainland.

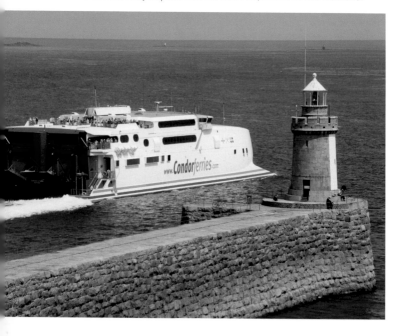

Emergencies

Dial 999 for police, fire, ambulance or coastal rescue services. The Princess Elizabeth Hospital, at Le Vauquiedor, St Martin, Guernsey (tel: 01481-725 241), has a 24-hour emergency unit. There is no longer a reciprocal health agreement between Guernsey and the UK and hospital treatment is charged for, with a very limited number of exemptions. Primary care doctors and dentists are in private practice and all patients are required to pay for treatment. Comprehensive medical insurance is therefore strongly recommended.

Herm has no medical facilities, though helicopter-borne emergency services are available. Sark has a Medical Centre opposite the New Island Hall (tel: 01481-832 045, or in an emergency telephone 07781100815). Alderney has the small Mignot Memorial Hospital (tel: 01481-822 822) and a Medical Centre at Sundial House, Les Rocquettes (tel: 01481-822 077).

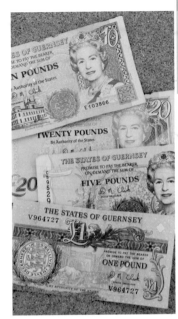

Above: the Guernsey pound is legal tender on the islands only.

Money

Sterling is the currency of the island. Guernsey also has its own currency, in the same denominations as UK notes and coins, apart from the fact that it still has £1 notes. UK and Guernsey currency can be used within the islands but Channel Island sterling will not be accepted in the UK apart from in banks, which will exchange notes. Some shops will accept euros, although change will generally be given in sterling. All major debit and credit cards are widely accepted throughout the islands. ATM machines can be found at most of the high street banks in St Peter Port, the airport, some supermarkets, garages and out of town banks throughout the island. Sark has no ATMs.

The lack of VAT and low duty on imported luxury items is mainly offset by the higher transport costs.

Opening times

Bank, shop and post office opening times are the same as those of the UK. Most museums and tourist attractions are open from 9am or 10am to 5pm from April to October, with some of the major sites open all year. For a list of current openings visit the Guernsey Tourism website (www.visitguernsey.com). In Guernsey pubs are normally open Monday to Saturday from 11am until late, with slightly shorter hours on a Sunday.

Telephones

Most mobiles will work on the islands but some networks require a roaming facility plus international dialling code. Pay-as-you-go phones only operate where there is an agreement with the network provider. Check with your service provider prior to departure.

Above: the Tourist Information Centre in Guernsey will help plan your trip.

The code for Guernsey, Herm, Sark and Alderney is 01481 from the UK and +44 1481 internationally. Although the code appears to be a UK one, the Channel Islands are excluded from the UK national price rates and the costs of calls are similar to those for Europe. Many hotels offer WiFi,

Above: public phone boxes.

sometimes chargeable. Free WiFi hotspots include Guernsey Airport, the Tourist Information office, Guille-Alles Library and some cafés.

Tourist information

Guernsey Information Centre (North Esplanade, St Peter Port tel: 01481-723 552; www.visitguernsey.com) has a wealth of information on the island and can also arrange accommodation during your visit. For information on the other three islands contact:

Herm Tourism (tel: 01481-722377, www.herm.com).

Sark Tourism, The Avenue, Sark, (tel: 01481-832 345; www.sark.com).

Alderney Tourism, 51 Victoria Street, St Anne, Alderney (tel: 01481-822 811; www.visitalderney.com).

Entertainment

To find out what's on locally, pick up the monthly *Diary of Events* from the

Information Centre (also available online at www.visitguenrsey.com) or go to www.guernseytickets.gg. The *St James Diary* lists poetry readings, art exhibitions, concerts and lectures hosted by St James, the church in College Street, St Peter Port, which now forms Guernsey's premier arts venue (www.stjames.gg).

Guernsey has a small, four-screen cinema showing new releases, near the airport at the Mallard Complex, La Villiaze Road, Forest (www.mallard cinema.co.uk). Alderney has a small cinema on Victoria Street, St Anne.

The Doghouse, Rohais, St Peter Port (www.doghouse.gg) is the best venue in town for live entertainment, with live music most nights, plus monthly UK tribute bands.

The oldest nightclub on Guernsey (and some say still the best) is Les Folies d'Amour, North Plantation, St Peter Port , but most of the action takes place on Le Pollet: Barbados Beach Club has a fun tropical atmosphere; the newer Fusion (www.fusion. gg), has weekly live entertainment and RED (www.red.gg) has a harbour view and a great list of cocktails.

Travel Documents and Customs Allowances

Although a passport isn't necessary for visitors arriving from the British Isles or the Republic of Ireland, airlines do require photo ID. A passport is required if you visit France.

Guernsey is not part of the EU, so you can buy duty-free goods when travelling to and from the island. Maximum allowances are 200 cigarettes or 100 cigarillos or 50 cigars or 250 grams of tobacco; 4 litres of still table wine; 1 litre of spirits or strong liqueurs over 22 percent volume or two litres of fortified wine, sparkling wine or other liqueurs; 50 litres of beer or cider; £390-worth of other goods including perfume, jewellery and gifts.

Below: live entertainment sometimes spills onto the streets in St Peter Port.

Accommodation

From simple B&Bs to stylishly converted farmhouses and chic boutique hotels, Guernsey offers accommodation to cater for most tastes.

Accommodation is plentiful but you won't find many bargains, especially if you book your hotel independently of transport. The best deals are the packages which include air or sea transport. Many of the hotels offer this option on their websites; alternatively you can do it through specialist operators. For example, Island Getaways (tel: 01983 721111; www.island getaways.co.uk) offer spring deals whereby the total cost for a week's holiday in a 3-star hotel, travel included (and car hire if you pay in advance) is less than the cost of accommodation alone booked through the hotel. Rates are amost invariably cheaper off-season and there are some great deals at the hotels that remain open in winter. For rooms in July and August book well ahead. Supplements are usually charged for seaview rooms; it's often worth the extra per night for the fabulous view you wake up to.

The Guernsey Tourist Board brochure (available online at www.visit guernsey.com) has a comprehensive illustrated section on accommodation available on the islands of Guernsey, Herm, Sark and Alderney. The website will also give you the latest tour operator deals. Tour companies specialising in Guernsey include Premier Holidays (tel: 0844-493 7529; www. premierholidays.co.uk/guernsey), Channel Islands' Direct (tel: 0844-470 4937510; www.channelislands direct.co.uk) and Discover Guernsey

Below: the Braye Beach Hotel offers excellent views over the sands.

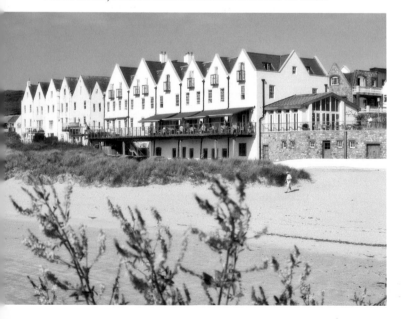

(tel: 0844-415 6653); www.guernsey travel.com)

St Peter Port offers the best sight-seeing, shopping and choice of restaurants. Buses from here will take you all over the island; it is also convenient for hopping across to Herm or Sark. Alternatively there are attractive beach hotels, and converted farmhouses and manor houses inland.

Old-fashioned values are still often adhered to, but that doesn't mean you won't get WiFi or power showers in the upper bracket hotels. Guernsey now has its first 5-star hotel, the Old Government House Hotel & Spa, and many of the 4-stars have undergone stylish revamps in the last few years.

Most places will require credit card details before confirming a reservation, and for special deals you may need to pay in full prior to arrival. VAT is not chargeable in the Channel Islands.

Above: Le Pollet, Guernsey's cobbled shopping street.

Hotels, self catering and camping
The price bands below are a guideline for the cost of a standard double room and breakfast for two in high season.

£££	over £200
££	£110–200
£	under £110

GUERNSEY
The Bay Apartments
Vale, tel: 07781-145 129; www.thebay guernsey.co.uk. Spotless self-catering apartments with spectacular views of the sandy Pembroke Bay. All apartments have sea views apart from one. Facilities include tennis, indoor swimming pool and health and beauty salon. Convenient for golfers with L'Ancresse golf club nearby. £750–£1,400 per week depending on size.

Bella Luce Hotel
La Fosse, St Martin, GY4 6EB, tel: 01481-238 764; www.bellalucehotel. com. This ancient manor house has been transformed into a luxury bou-tique hotel. Colonial-style decor, top-quality food, swimming pool and popular Bella Bar and Grill. **££**

Best Western Hotel de Havelet
Havelet, St Peter Port, GY1 1BA; tel: 01481-722 199; www.dehavelet guernsey.com. Georgian house on a hill with fine views of the harbour and islands. It is a 15-minute walk uphill from the centre of St Peter Port – or you can take the courtesy minibus which links the hotel and town centre several times a day in summer. Indoor pool with sauna, steam room and jacuzzi. **££**

Bon Port Hotel
Rue des Clotures, St Martins, GY4 6EW, tel: 01481-239 249; www.bon port.com. The only hotel to overlook the beautiful Moulin Huet Bay and famous 'Pea Stacks', which were immortalised by Renoir. Tasteful en suite bedrooms, heated outdoor swimming pool, gym and sauna. **££**

Cobo Bay Hotel
Cobo, Castel, GY5 7HB, tel: 01481-257 102; www.cobobayhotel.com.

Ideal beach holiday hotel with excellent value rooms opposite sandy Cobo Bay. Award-winning restaurant. Small complimentary health suite. **££**

Duke of Richmond Hotel

Cambridge Park, St Peter Port, GY1 1UY, tel: 01481-726 221; www.dukeof richmond.com. This comfy 4-star hotel beside Candie Gardens has been extensively refurbished and taken on a contemporary look with a black and white lounge and a Leopard Bar/Restaurant with bold stripes and 'leopard-skin' fabrics. Guest room prices vary substantially depending on the degree of luxury (there's a Penthouse and three Junior suites) and the views – many overlook the sea. **££–£££**

The Farmhouse

Route des Bas Courtils, St Saviour, GY7 9YF; tel: 01481-264 181; www. thefarmhouse.gg. Run by the Nuss-baumer family for three generations this farmhouse, converted to a 4-star

Below: La Frégate Hotel.

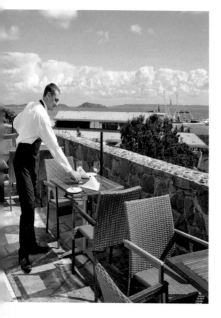

hotel, is among Guernsey's favourite hotels. The 14 bedrooms are furnished in contemporary style, with large walk-in showers. Popular restaurant with meals available by the fire, poolside or in one of the gazebos. **££**

Fauquets Valley Campsite

Candie Road, Castel, GY5 7QAL, tel: 01481-255 460; www.fauxquets.co.uk. Wonderful campsite in a tranquil valley. All amenities including heated pool, licensed restaurant and bar, shop and children's playground and games room. **£**

Fleur du Jardin

Kings Mills, Castel, GY5 7JT, tel: 01481-257 996; www.fleurdujardin. com. Named after a breed of Guernsey cow, this old farmhouse has been stylishly renovated and offers rooms with bleached timber walls and sandstone bathrooms. First-class gastro-pub food, solar-heated pool and new health suite. **££**

Hotel La Michele

Les Hubits de Bas, St Martins, GY4 6NB, tel: 01481-238 065; www.la michelehotel.com. This small family-run hotel is renowned for hospitality. Restaurant, bar and attractive heated outdoor swimming pool in secluded gardens. **£**

La Frégate Hotel

Les Cotils, St Peter Port, GY1 1UT, tel: 01481-724 624; www.lafregatehotel. com. Stylish, deluxe boutique hotel in its own grounds in St Peter Port. Fantastic views across the islands and one of the best restaurants in Guernsey (see page 29). **£££**

Mille Fleurs Self Catering

Rue du Bordage, St Pierre du Bois, GY7 9DW, tel: 01481-263 911; www.mille fleurs.co.uk. Comfortable self-catering cottages set in a peaceful rural location with internationally acclaimed gardens. Heated outdoor swimming pool. Open all year. £870–2,150 per week depending on size and season. **£–££**

Above: when booking at the White House Hotel, ask for a room with a sea view.

The Old Government House Hotel & Spa

St Ann's Place, St Peter Port, GY1 2NU; tel: 01481-724 921, www.the oghhotel.com. The former official residence of Guernsey's governor, the OGH (as it's familiarly known) dates from 1858 and has recently been extensively refurbished and upgraded. This is the only five-star hotel on the island. Expect plush bedrooms, top-notch cuisine in the Brasserie or Curry Room, traditional afternoon teas and excellent service. Leisure facilities include a well-equipped spa, gym and outdoor heated pool. **£££**

HERM

White House Hotel, Herm, GY1 3HR, tel: 01481-750 075; www.herm. com. Ideal place to unwind away from the 21st century. Family run for over half a century with old-fashioned values, good service and excellent food and wine. Swimming pool, tennis court and croquet lawn. Holiday cottages, apartments, cabins and a camp-site with sea-facing terraces are also available. **££–£££**

SARK

Dixcart Bay Hotel

Sark, Channel Islands, GY10 1SD, tel: 01481-832 832; www.dixcartbay.sark islandhotels.com. Sark's oldest hotel has seen a major overhaul with a conservatory restaurant, cobbled courtyard and new apartments. A large garden merges with the wooded valley which winds down to Dixcart Bay. The hotel's Hugo's Bistro, open all day every day in season, is named after the French writer Victor Hugo who was an occasional resident here. Guests have use of facilities of the three other hotels in the Sark Island Hotels group (including the Petit Champ). **£££**

Hotel Petit Champ

Sark, Channel Islands, GY10 1SF, tel: 01481-832 832; www.hotelpetit champ.sarkislandhotels.com. A small hotel with unrivalled sea views and spectacular sunsets. Balcony rooms are the most sought after, with views of neighbouring Herm, Jethou and Guernsey. The restaurant has a good local reputation, serving fresh Sark seafood and locally reared beef, lamb and port. Solar-heated swimming pool, croquet lawn and alfresco lunches. **££**

La Sablonnerie

Sark, Channel Islands, GY10 1SD, tel: 01481-832 061; www.lasablonnerie. com. A total escape – located on Little Sark, this remote farmhouse hotel is reached by the owner's horse-drawn carriages and offers rural tranquillity, plus excellent cuisine and comfortable rooms. One of the loveliest hotels on the Channel Islands. **££**

ALDERNEY

Braye Beach Hotel, Braye Street, GY9 3XT; tel: 01481-824 300; www. brayebeach.com. Chic designer hotel with a perfect setting overlooking Braye Beach. All rooms have bathrobes, a complimentary decanter of sherry, fresh fruit on arrival and free-

WiFi. Book ahead for sea view rooms. The company also owns Blue Islands airline; you can find some excellent package deals. For the restaurant, *see page 105*. **££–£££**

Farm Court

Le Petit Val, Alderney, GY9 3UX, tel: 01481-822 075; www.farmcourt-alderney.co.uk. B&B in small converted barns, generous breakfasts, plus an owner who gives painting lessons. Self-catering also available. Good value for money. **£**

Fort Clonque

The Landmark Trust, Shottesbrooke, Maidenhead, Berkshire, SL6 3SW, tel: 01628-825 925; www.landmarktrust. org.uk. Built in the 1840s, Fort Clonque is cut off from Alderney at high tide. The fort has been converted to surprisingly comfortable self-catering accommodation, with sleeping quarters for up to 13 people (or 14 if you count the ghost), in four different buildings. Four nights from £655.

Below: La Sablonnerie hotel uses produce from its farm and gardens.

Index

Credits

Insight Great Breaks Guernsey
Written and updated by: Susie Boulton
Edited by: Catherine Dreghorn
Picture Researcher: Jo Mercer
Picture Manager: Zoë Goodwin
Maps: APA Publications
Production: Tynan Dean and Rebeka Davies
Publishing Manager: Rachel Fox
Series Editor: Sarah Clark

All images by Mockford and Bonetti/ Apa Publications except; Courtesy Caragh Chocolates 92C; The Guernsey Press Co Ltd 53B; Flydime 109B; La Fregate 124; Vist Guernsey 4BR, 5BR/CR/TL, 7B, 8T, 9B, 11, 19B, 24/T, 25B, 6B, 28B, 30/31, 30B, 31C/T, 37B, 38T, 41, 42T, 43, 44, 45, 47B, 48, 51C, 59B, 67B, 70/T, 74/T, 76, 77, 79, 80T, 85T, 86, 88/T, 90B, 91/T, 93T, 96, 97T, 98/99, 100, 104B, 106/107, 110T, 113/T, 114, 115, 116, 120, 121, 122, 125, 126

Cover pictures by: Colour Library, iStock-photo and Mockford and Bonetti/Apa

CONTACTING THE EDITORS: As every effort is made to provide accurate information in this publication, we would appreciate it if readers would call our attention to any errors and omissions by contacting:
Apa Publications, PO Box 7910, London SE1 1WE, England.
Email: insight@apaguide.co.uk

Information has been obtained from sources believed to be reliable, but its accuracy and completeness, and the opinions based thereon, are not guaranteed.

© 2014 APA Publications (UK) Ltd.
Second Edition 2014; Reprinted 2014
Printed in China by CTPS

Map Production: Apa Cartography Department.

Worldwide distribution enquiries:
APA Publications GmbH & Co. Verlag KG (Singapore branch)
7030 Ang Mo Kio Ave 5
08-65 Northstar @ AMK
Singapore 569880
apasin@singnet.com.sg

Distributed in the UK and Ireland by:
Dorling Kindersley Ltd (a Penguin Group company)
80 Strand, London, WC2R 0RL, UK
sales@uk.dk.com

INSIGHT GUIDES

INSPIRING YOUR NEXT ADVENTURE

Insight Guides offers you a range of travel guides
to match your needs. Whether you are looking for
inspiration for planning a trip, cultural information,
walks and tours, great listings, or practical advice, we
have a product

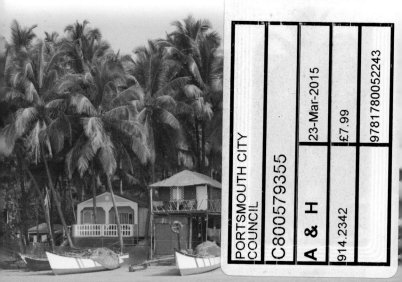

www.insightguides.com